# THE CHORBA TRAIL

## By

## Jerry Brian Riess

*The Chorba Trail*
by Jerry Brian Riess

Printed in the United States of America

ISBN 9781615795123

Unless otherwise indicated, Bible Quotations are taken from The King James Version of the Bible. Public Domain

www.xulonpress.com

Dedicated in love to my daughter
Maria Lynn and my son
Jerry Brian in hopes
they both find the same eternal
Joy I have in Jesus

# Preface

Some may wonder why I would choose to write about personal matters, some embarrassing and others revealing weaknesses of a private nature. There is no question this book presents wounds and hurts that normally would be shut away. But there is a triumph of Spirit, and an insight into a caring and loving God that I feel compelled to tell. I want to shout from the hills, what the Lord has done in my life.

For me to fail to tell the whole story would be to deny God His righteous Glory. His work in my life is complete. He carried me from the very beginning of time. He had His hand on me through all of the years of sorrow. He has borne my transgressions, and my pain.

I have taken care to disguise some places and names of people so as to not embarrass anyone. There is also the fear of retaliation by some in positions of authority so I have also changed locations, dates and participants. The book is not intended to be historically accurate in every respect. Rather, it reflects what I was told or led to believe by others. My intention is to reflect their subjective understandings and my responses to those understandings, rather than a historical narrative. This is written not as an act of revenge, criticism or self-pity, but hopefully as an example to others that you can never sell God short. You cannot out-give God, and you cannot re-pay God. The price is too heavy. He never gives up on you, no matter what you do. All you can do is respond to God and love Him for who He is. Place your heart, cares and life in the hands of the one person who purely loves you! The rewards are eternal and the other option is unacceptable.

To list all of those to whom I am indebted would not be possible. Literally hundreds of people on five continents have been a big part in bringing life to this ministry and work. As of this writing, we are assembling 10,000 candy packs for distribution this spring. New to the handout bags for 3rd world children are wooden cars each hand made by "Toys for God's Kids," a mens group of volunteers from Denver to Seattle. Last week we wired $400 needed to rebuild the house of a man in Narsapur, India which was destroyed by a cyclone. An inoculation program and Caleb medical mission is being conducted for four days in Enugu, Nigeria at a cost of $1200.00. Two army doctors and two nurses are assisting the outreach, being financed by a gift to Caleb Ministries from Heart of God Fellowship as a thank you for our contributions to their work in Abra, Philippines. A grant of $1500.00 was sent to Grace and Mercy Ministry Missions in Hanuman Junction, India and another of $1500.00 to Sea Coast Ministries in Kothapatnam, India, for buying rice, bibles, blankets and sponsoring Vacation Bible Schools. In Romania, work is being completed by Caleb Ministries on the Pecka Psychiatric Hospital and in a Youth Camp south of Braila, all with funds raised by Caleb Churches in Romania. Braille Bibles are being distributed in Romania, Moldova and The Ukraine, street kids are being provided food, medical care, clothes and counseling, and new churches are being founded in remote villages and big cities. A new Kitchen and restrooms have been completed from our grant at Saint Esteban Church in The Philippines. Three new Caleb churches have been started in Belize and a fourth is being seeded now in Mexico by Bishop Marben Lagmay. Books are being collected for two Philippine Seminaries, medicines being catalogued for shipping to Bulgaria, Russia, Romania, Nigeria and The Philippines, and young people are attending school and college on Caleb Grants in four countries.

Only by the Grace of God and literally hundreds of volunteers, prayer partners and contributors would this be possible.

This book is dedicated to all those who helped along the way. The man who gave 50 cents at the Bread of Life Mission, the school girl who earned $12 selling cards, the second grader donating his $2.00 savings, the helping hands who assembled thousands of candy packs, and those hardy souls who came to load 170 high-cube forty-foot containers at our warehouse. I love you one and all!

The Title was selected carefully with particular attention to several points: Caleb Good News Ministries has been the benefactor of many who went before it preaching Gods Word and sowing seeds. Ours has been a ministry of bring together people and giving opportunity for their declaration of faith. It is The Holy Spirit which reveals Christ and only The Holy Spirit. The Chorba Trail is appropriate as a description because Chorba soup or stew by its nature is a potpourri of ingredients based upon what is and was available, just as Caleb Good News Ministries is an opportunistic evangelism adapting itself to resources and needs available at the right time and place. Romania is the true birthplace for this unique ministry as that is where we grew and found our wings!

1 Cor 15:24-28

²⁴Then cometh the end, when he shall have delivered up the kingdom to God, even the Father; when he shall have put down all rule and all authority and power.

²⁵ For he must reign, till he hath put all enemies under his feet.

²⁶ The last enemy that shall be destroyed is death.

²⁷ For he hath put all things under his feet. But when he saith, all things are put under him, it is manifest that he is excepted, which did put all things under him.

²⁸ And when all things shall be subdued unto him, then shall the Son also himself be subject unto him that put all things under him, that God may be all in all.

KJV

# Chapter 1

# AN INEVITABLE DEPRESSION-ERA MARRIAGE OF EXPEDIENCY

*Gen 2:7*

*7 And the Lord God formed man of the dust of the ground, and breathed into his nostrils the breath of life; and man became a living soul.*
*KJV*

In a shabby one bedroom house near Youngstown steel company, at the foot of Seattle's' Elliot bay, I came into this world on a cold December morning in 1939. Dad worked nights at Boeing as a riveter, a far cry from his earlier years in Los Angeles where he was a young boxer making a reputation for himself in the sports community. Our little rented house was very crowded with three older brothers, Henry, Charles and Butch. Youngstown was but one step above a shanty town, supplying laborers for the steel mill and Seattle shipyards in a struggling economy. A small wood stove in the corner provided the only heat. One Christmas, the family felt fortunate to have five dollars to splurge. Mother cooked up a black skillet of hamburger meat, and we had a feast of hamburger, boiled potatoes, peas, and pumpkin pie. Butch was in the high chair, saying 'dabum' or 'tank you'. The scrawny little Christmas tree stood about 3' high, with some colored paper ornaments. Charles and Henry played with a little ice truck that we shared as our Christmas. It had a glass cube of ice, and little ice tongs.

The neighbors knew little about the family, and we kept pretty much to ourselves, having fled San Diego not many months before. Henry and Charles were living in Juarez Mexico, barely a year before that. Their natural father, Henry Walker, had kidnapped them and hidden them in Juarez from mother years before. Walker was fleeing from the authorities, following a gunfight on the streets of San Diego. A relationship of convenience came about when my father designated himself as the protector and provider for mother though she had rejected his romantic advances for over a year. Pregnant with my brother Butch and desperate to recover her two older boys, she gave in to his advances and they formed an imperfect but workable family unit. He clearly loved her and pursued her, waiting flowers in hand on the stoop each day as she came home from her work as a social worker. When she had to be hospitalized with the birth of Butch, he arrived at her bedside with a turtle named "Myrtle", and she was won over to his care and protection, having few other options.

Both parents found themselves at odds with their own families, having elected to pursue lives independent of their parent's dreams. Raised in St. Paul's Episcopal boarding school in Walla Walla, far from her wealthy family in Butte Montana, mother followed her romantic dreams and defied her parents, by running off with a young rodeo star at age 17. The marriage to Henry Walker turned sour after the birth of the older boys Henry and Charles. He became more interested in serving the Communist party and its endeavors to overthrow the government of the United States than in caring for his young family. The participation in cell meetings, and droning anti-American rhetoric drove my mother to turn him in to the authorities with evidence of his illegal activities, resulting in the San Diego gunfight and his kidnapping of the two older boys.

Dad was raised in a wealthy setting in Los Angeles, the only boy in a family with three older sisters. He became a golden gloves boxer, much to the chagrin of his family. The disreputable nature of his chosen profession left him at odds with the entire family and at age 17, he suffered a severe beating. He was no longer able to compete further in the arena he so loved. He rode stage between Tijuana and San Diego as "shotgun" for several years and then found work as a mechanic, welder, inventor, and handyman. His near-genius mind suited him to any number of endeavors as he became well-trained in diverse talents. He married his high school sweetheart Francis, but sadly, she was killed in an automobile accident less than a year later.

In 1937 these two, Alice Jane Walker and Allen Lewis Riess, refugees from wealth and social status, found each other having common ground only in their being rejected by their very families and their loss or betrayal by loved ones. It was more out of persistence than love, that they formed a partnership and family. Though my father deeply loved my mother, she found him more useful and helpful than love-able. It is clear that Butch was fathered neither by Henry Walker, nor my dad. He was probably conceived before they connected as a family and his presence undoubtedly influenced mother to accept the advances of my dad.

By June 1939, the older boys were found in Ciudad Juarez, Mexico, where they were being raised by a Mexican lady in a daycare. My parents contacted the San Diego authorities and obtained copies of the police reports, both as to Walker and their abduction.

Finally after three years. the two older boys were kidnapped back across the border to USA! Their identities were changed and relocation made to Seattle by their new "family" of six.

## Chapter 2

# TRANSITION TO YOUNGSTOWN

*Num 21:5-7*

*5 And the people spake against God, and against Moses, Wherefore have ye brought us up out of Egypt to die in the wilderness? for there is no bread, neither is there any water; and our soul loatheth this light bread.*

*6 And the Lord sent fiery serpents among the people, and they bit the people; and much people of Israel died.*

*7 Therefore the people came to Moses, and said, We have sinned, for we have spoken against the Lord, and against thee; pray unto the Lord, that he take away the serpents from us. And Moses prayed for the people.*

*KJV*

At age 26, my mother had birthed three children, was in her second marriage, cooking on a wood stove, and living in a shipyard slum area of Seattle. Our father Allen was seemingly the best thing that ever happened to the family. He did the best he could for us, and fortunately for us, he was an incredibly skilled mechanic, and wood worker. He had a great job with Boeing, as they introduced the war horse B-17, in 1939. He slept on the couch during the days, while working swing shift. Little in the household resembled a traditional marriage as both parents worked and led separate lives except as dictated by family needs. In late 1938, we moved from the house in 'Youngstown, ' (called that because of the nearby steel mill), to a farm house in Kirkland. The Youngstown House was simply too small for four children, since she was pregnant again. My dad desired a place to work on cars for extra income but if was not feasible in the small home.

In Kirkland, we had a two story farmhouse with many rooms. There were pigs, goats, ducks, and chickens. The farmer across the road behind us brought us a pail of fresh milk twice a week, and showed us how to butcher hogs. We had a big orchard, with many fruit trees. Mother's Springer Spaniel, Suzy, had to be put down, because we couldn't afford to take her to a vet when she became ill. We had a large circular drive lined with stones, which the older boys had to whitewash. Mother milked the goat, named "Plenty", because she gave lots of milk, to make cheese and cottage cheese. But in time we couldn't afford the farm house, and had to again move. Begrudgingly, Moms' father came to the rescue and purchased a fruit tree farm in Gregory Heights for $5,000 in 1940, as a gift to the family, but keeping title in his name, having little faith in his wayward daughter and no trust in her new companion 'husband'. Sadly, the four surrounding lots were sold off for bills and taxes, and the farm fell into disrepair because of the inability of our family to farm it. Originally the home was rather stately, but it soon became a graveyard for automobiles under repair, various types of junk acquired by my father, and lack of attention to the yard and gardens. Seven years later we needed to mortgage the house itself but grandpa insisted first there be a proper marriage. So, at seven years of age, I became (ring bearer) at my parents wedding in Vancouver, Washington. The remaining interest in the house was then deeded over to my mother, starting a string of many years of delinquent tax payments, disrepair and maintenance neglect.

A big farm house, it was situated thirteen miles from Seattle and 3 miles from the village of Burien. There were only four other homes in the Gregory Heights area, each being separated by brush and trees. The yard was frequently visited by coyotes, raccoons, chicken hawks and even deer. The roads for the last mile to the farm were little more than gravel and rocks. Visitors were infrequent in our area. There was a very large garage that would accommodate three cars and a workbench on the ground level. A second story on the garage contained a bedroom, kitchen and dining area. The third level was a pigeon coup! We had a cow, rabbits, chickens, pigeons and a big garden surrounded by fruit trees. A neighbor pastured their horse 'Pep'. It would appear to be a paradise for four young boys, but never lived up to that dream.

Apart from the fact that there was little affection shown between the parents, the four boys always appeared to be at odds with each other. As the youngest and the only child of the father figure, I was resented and shunned by the older boys. Henry and Charles were an inseparable pair, both athletic and adventuresome. Their bond had obviously formed years before, probably while in Mexico, and the younger boys were unwelcome in their world. I was a sickly child, rheumatic fever among other things, and unable to keep up with the activities of my siblings. This became a point of resentment and abandonment. Our parents worked most weekends, leaving us to our own devices. Henry and Charles would go fishing or camping or hunting, but I was considered too young and too ill to participate in such activities. I was unable to run or exert myself much physically, a condition that haunted me the rest of my life. To prevent my coming along when my brothers wanted to play, they used to tied me to the apple tree in the backyard, where I would remain all day. On those days when my mother came home first and found me tied to the tree I was scolded for aggravating my older brothers. When I would complain, they would take away my clothes when next they tie me to the tree! Somehow, my parents viewed this is a toughening tactic, and simply did not want to get involved. "Boys will be boys".... Complaints only resulted in everyone getting punished, and this grew the resentment more for the next episode.

Clearly, we struggled financially in the early years of World War II, and it was always a frustration to get sufficient ration stamps for meat, sugar, gasoline or shoes. We grew most of our food on our abbreviated farm. I recall one day when my father brought home four large crates of radishes that had apparently been dumped out by a restaurant or farmer. My brother Butch and I were assigned to scrape off the slime and wash the radishes and save the ones that were still firm. I recall our sitting behind the garage in the sunlight doing this disgusting job and vowing never to eat a radish again as long as we lived. Being the youngest, my clothes consisted mostly of what my brothers had worn out or outgrown. Because I had been become fat, probably eating out of frustration, I was often put on a diet to no effect. My meals were served with a discourse on the number of calories involved in each item. My father resorted to shaming me as a way of trying to get me to lose weight, giving me the nickname "Lardo" around the house, which my brothers gladly spread to the schoolyard. I was deeply embarrassed and humiliated, hating to go to school and face the other children. To make matters worse, I often was given my father's trousers and shirts to wear, because there were no other large clothes available. I would wrap the trousers around myself and tie them with a rope, resulting in more chiding and embarrassment at school!

My father was always concerned that the older boys not resent me as his only son. He took extra effort to appear to be fair, sometimes leaving me with the short end of the stick. I recall one day when he came home with three lollipops to divide between four boys. I was left with none. I was not told that he was not their father until years later and could not understand why he favored them over me. It was very confusing, because I did not understand what I had done wrong that he would treat them different from me.

My dad was quick tempered, and very impatient. I do not believe he was comfortable in the role of being a parent.

From my earliest years I had little relationship with my mother. She left for work each morning, taking the bus or being driven by my dad to the Army Corps of Engineers and later to the General services administration, where she worked in financial services. When she came home from work, she usually went to the bedroom with a can or two of beer and spent the evening there. Father said that she was very tired or sick, and that we should not be concerned. As a consequence, my father and I prepared most of the meals and we ate at the kitchen breakfast nook. He used metal trays he got at the surplus store for our meals, reserving the dining room and china for special times only. It was difficult working with my father because he was so intolerant and could be brought to violence easily. When I was about five he came home from work and discovered a package of Ritz crackers was missing from the kitchen cupboard. They were my mother's favorite crackers, and my brothers and I all knew that she had eaten them earlier. However, the level of anger was so high that we were afraid to tell him. He lined the four of us up in a row in the basement and demanded of each of us which one ate the crackers. The oldest, Henry, said no he did not eat the crackers. The second, Charles, said he did not eat the crackers; Butch and I followed in order denying that we either one of us had even seen the crackers. My father grabbed a 2 x 4 and began to beat all four of us until his anger subsided. He struck me in the right ear so hard that I still have hearing loss to this day.

A few years later, my brother Butch and I decided to go to church. We had been warned by my father and mother to stay away from church as it was not a place for us. My father declared that the church was part of the Communist conspiracy to brainwash us and we should have nothing to do with it. Being curious, Butch and I took off in our bicycles early one Sunday morning and went to the Catholic Church. However, the priest met us at the door and told us that we could not come in and we should go home and come back with our parents. We returned home dejected and confused, but keeping to ourselves about our experience. The next day, someone told my father that we had been seen at the Catholic Church and he came home furious. He grabbed a stick and started whipping both of us. I had a Llewellyn Setter named "Putt" who was my constant companion. Putt came to my defense and grabbed the stick with his jaw, only to have my father's wrath turned upon him. My dad beat the dog to death in front of us. He clubbed the dog in the head over and over until it was like red mush! Then ordered us to get a shovel and bury the dog in the backyard, not telling anyone what happened.

On another occasion my father was giving his haircuts in the kitchen when he cut my left ear, severely. I was bleeding and crying as he poured cold water on it to help it clot. Once it stopped the bleeding he blamed me for not sitting still and ordered me to clean up the kitchen. I could not understand why I was to blame, and why I was being punished. For years I dreaded haircuts!

My mother was living most of her existence in the bedroom or at work and her drinking became more pronounced. It was becoming an embarrassment to be seen with her anywhere in public. And I shuddered whenever I had to bring a note home from school asking for my parents to come for a conference or meeting. Fortunately, they ignored most of the notes and rarely if ever showed up at the school.

When we moved into the Gregory Heights house, there were large Persian rugs in the living room and dining room. I used to spend hours at play with my "toy cars" tracing the patterns around the rugs. My toy cars were the metal beer can openers that came in each 24 package of Alt Heidelberg or Olympia beer before the days of pop top cans. I had a shoebox in which I collected the openers and kept them as my cars, separated by the various designs on the openers themselves. At one time I had over 300 in my collection, and I was very proud of it.

My brother Butch and I once more tried to attend a church when I was seven, being curious as to what went on inside of those buildings. The people seem so happy when they came out, and there were notices about dinners and social events on the lawns that made us curious. Our family went very few places and we wanted to know more about the rest of the world. Early Sunday morning, we rode our bikes down to the local Presbyterian Church. I grant that we were rather shabbily dressed, and probably looked unkempt. We entered the church, and sat down quietly in a row in the back. We were behaving and were curious about the small plastic cups of juice and crackers. Suddenly, a man grabbed me by the back of the neck and took me to the door and pushed me out saying not to come back, that we were dirty. On the other side of the building, I found my brother Butch having been tossed out of the other doorway. I was very confused but knew for certain that I was not welcome in that church either. My dad never found out about that episode.

In 1949, the family found itself desperately in need of a car. All of the vehicles we had, and there was a large selection in the yard, did not work. My father was now engaged in real estate business, and my mother working for the General Services Administration. One day my father came home with a new white Ford. He had made arrangements with Ed Short Tractor Company to assemble 600 Simar Rototiller's in exchange for the money for the car. The following Saturday morning the entire family was gathered together at 7 a.m. and we all proceeded to a warehouse in Georgetown, where we begin the process of building Simar Rototiller's. As the youngest, my job was to sort out the burlap sacks of wheel lugs and to separate them by size, and to insert the bolts and nuts for attaching them to a metal wheel frame. I was attracted to the paint dipping pool, but constantly ushered back to the burlap sacks in the corner. My brother Butch was in charge of sorting engine parts and brothers Henry and Charles were involved in assembling the frames and handlebars. My father worked on the Briggs and Stratton engines along with my mother. We listened to Leo Lasson broadcasting the Seattle Rainier baseball games and lunched on day-old maple bars and donuts from Hanson's bakery. It took Saturday and Sunday's every week for the next 18 months for us to build the 600 tractors to pay off the car. The only weekend we did not work other than Christmas vacation, was the week before Thanksgiving, because my mother objected and my father consented, knowing her parents were coming up for the weekend from Portland for a short visit.

On four occasions, including that one, my grandfather came up for a visit from Portland. He would meet us at the Green Parrot Restaurant on Highway 99 in Midway, and he would buy a family style chicken dinner for our holiday treat. I do not recall him ever coming to our home, or any other visits with him other than at the restaurant. After dinner he would give us each our Christmas present in advance from the trunk of his car, usually a pair of pajamas and two pairs of socks. On one occasion, my father's parents came for a visit from Los Angeles and he and his wife drove us four boys around in his car for about an hour. It was a LaSalle Car with "jump seats" in the back. He drove us to see construction under way at what eventually would be Seattle Tacoma International Airport. That was the only contact I had with any grandparents that I can recall during my childhood.

Butch and I decided not to seek a church home any further. We talked about it a lot, being curious by the signs at the Catholic Church Friday's inviting people to a free Spaghetti Dinner but we were not wanted there. Butch and I grew close and looked after each other as best we could. We would spend the afternoon's sitting on the roof of the porch of the house watching the roadway for my father's return home from work. Sometimes we discussed ways to do him in, and sometimes we directed our attention to running away from home. No matter where we turned, life seemed a dead end to us. The older boys were involved with friends at school and could get rides from their buddies to go places and get away from the anger and uncertainty. We had little avenue of escape. The radio was our entertainment and on weekends we hauled beer bottles in my wagon down to Burien Tradewell where we got 2 cents for stubbies and 5 cents for quarts which we used to go to the matinee at the Den Burien Theater. If Butch sneaked in the back door, we had enough for popcorn!

I wanted very much to join the Cub Scouts, because my oldest brother had been in scouts for years. I was very proud of his accomplishments. I was enrolled in a Cub Scout pack, but at the second meeting the den mother said it was my turn to bring cookies for the next meeting. When I told my mother, she said there was no money for such things and I was no longer permitted to go to scouts.

In the summer months, my father erected a large ten by ten tent in the backyard, and set up army cots with army blankets for the four boys to sleep outdoors. We were not permitted in the house in the summer months, except in the kitchen for our dinner. It was very rare for us to even enter the living room or dining room area, and even more rare to see our mother. The tent experience was fun, because my older brothers were there and I was not scared. We would venture out at night, stealing food from neighbors' gardens and prowling through yards miles away from our home. However, one night a man came out from his house and started firing at us. My brothers ran off and left me and I walked on home slowly with my bottom full of buckshot. I was shattered that they would run off and leave me and learned never to trust them again. I expected a whipping but it didn't happen. Instead, Dad took me to the doctor and then to visit a policeman friend of his where I was duly warned against any future prowling at night! Nothing was said by me about my brother's involvement but I am sure dad knew. In September my oldest brother Henry had left to join the Navy.

My father acquired a parcel of real estate that we called the 'four acres' located in Midway, about 15 miles from our house. There was a huge old barn on the property and a farmhouse that had been badly neglected, and a well. The rest of the property was simply brush and trees that had been overgrown for years. Dad started a business called Diamond-Dowell Fence Company. He made pre-fabricated sections of fencing using rejected broomstick handles he bought from a broom company in Tacoma. The fence sections were in eight-foot and 6 foot lengths with the broomsticks in criss-cross pattern in the frame. Setting up business in the barn, he made the frames and stacked them in the corner. In June when school was out, my brother Butch and I were sent out to live in the barn and to put together the sections of fence by inserting the broomstick handles and painting the sections. My father left us with a small refrigerator, which had spaghetti and goulash in jars, boxes of cereal and canned evaporated milk to dilute. We had cans of sterno to heat the food in two pans he left with us. We had a bucket for getting water from the well about 500 feet away and soap for washing the dishes and ourselves. He provided us with sleeping bags to sleep on the floor and a small radio to listen to at night. I was nine and Butch was 10 1/2 years old. My father would visit us about every two weeks during the summer to see how we were doing and to create more frames for the fence. It was very scary and frightening to be left there. I hated it because it was very dark, cold at night, and the place was creepy with bugs, rats, and who knew what else. We use to cry ourselves to sleep or sit up and try to figure how to "do in" the old man, as we called him secretly. The only house nearby was about two blocks away, and the people were very unfriendly towards us. We tried to visit one evening, when they were holding a church service, but they chased us away. I recall listening to their singing from the woods, and how beautiful it sounded. But we were clearly unwelcome.

## Chapter 3

# THROWN TO THE FISH

*Ps 68:5-7*

*5 A father of the fatherless, and a judge of the widows,
is God in his holy habitation.
6 God setteth the solitary in families: he bringeth out
those which are bound with chains: but the rebellious dwell in a dry land.
KJV*

Many evenings were punctuated with bitter arguments and it was not uncommon to see mother with bruises and blackened eyes on the weekends. I use to look forward to Sundays because that meant a family dinner with mom and all of us listening to the radio together, but she didn't say much on those occasions. She had withdrawn pretty much into herself and into the books that she would obtain at the library on Saturday afternoons. I recall her coming home with a stack of 10 or 12 mystery novels, which kept her company during the week. During the winter months, she and dad would sit on their separate couches in the living room facing each other and drinking Olympia Beer or Alt Heidelberg until one or both fell asleep. I would play with my collection of metal beer can openers (before tab tops, one opener came free in each case!) pretending they were cars as I followed the pattern on the living room rug. (We were only permitted in the living room if both parents were there).

Henry would draw endlessly in charcoals and Charles carved model airplanes from balsa wood, from an old life raft we had acquired at the army-navy surplus store. We had a big supply of balsa wood as the raft was composed of cubes of balsa each covered in canvas and tar. Brother Butch and I listened to the radio together and at bedtime we four were sent upstairs, Henry and Charles to the big bedroom and Butch and I to the smaller one, They acted as a safe place because as much as my dad bellowed about coming up to "beat the living Jesus out of each of you", he rarely came up because the stairs were an ordeal for his 400+ pound frame.

Reason suggests we would hate my dad but in fact it was a combination of wanting him dead, planning his demise, and then realizing he was our provider. In his way he was the only parent I had. My brothers could escape by reflecting on their real dad but I was not so fortunate. He was the source of what food, shelter and protection I had. Since my brothers always emphasized not being not his kids, I had no choice but to see him as my imperfect parent.

In 1952 I completed the sixth grade at Lake Burien grade school. Clearly, the teachers noted that things were not right in our family, probably because of our apparel and shyness around other students and unwillingness to participate in social activities. On the last day of school, the principal announced over the public address system that I had been voted by the teachers as the student of the year for Lake Burien grade school. This was a big surprise and obviously a contrived event to help my low self esteem. I was asked to come to the office to receive my prize, which turned out to be a copy of Richard Halliburton's book, "The book of Marvels". It was a wonderful book, bound in green with full page photos of natural and man-made wonders about the world. Most of my teachers had written words of encouragement inside the cover. Obviously, they knew something was dreadfully wrong in my life and were trying to encourage me for the years to come. I treasured the book very much, which detailed the wonders of the world both natural and man-made. There were large photographs of many beautiful things in the world that I dreamed of one day seeing. Sadly, my father caught me daydreaming over the book and took it away telling me I would never amount to anything and would not see any of those beautiful sites. He burned the book in the fireplace. In 2009, some 57 years later, I found a copy of Richard Halliburton's book on the Internet and enjoy it to this day! The amazing thing for me is to realize how many of those sights the Lord has graciously permitted me to visit in my life.

I remember one summer day when dad returned from the 3 GIs' army surplus store, he had the eight metal trays we use for our meals, army boots for each of the four boys which left black marks on the floors in the house, pea jackets for winter, and a large box of canned goods with missing labels! It was always a surprise for dinner he said. From creamed corn and apple sauce to army stew and canned tomatoes, you never knew what you would have until the can was opened. It did no good to complain, because the choice was to have what was in the can or nothing. One time he brought home Montana Horsemeat. He fried it as patties and added a pineapple slice to cut the bitterness. It was awful!

Besides selling real estate, dad tried his hand at teaching night school in welding, making wood toys in his workshop, and trying to perfect many of his endless inventions. Mom was the only steady wage earner, working for the Department of the Army and later for General Services Administration in payroll accounting. Dad would drive her to the bus each morning and then pick her up at night, as she was not permitted by him to drive. He was convinced in his mind that she was very ill and needed constant monitoring. She was kept away from us in her bedroom most evenings when she came home from work. Dad would prepare the meals or we would make them ourselves. Through trial and error, I became the "cook" of the house from as long as I could remember.

When it came time to decide what to do for the summer my father announced he had a job for me. I was going to be a commercial fisherman. I was barely 11 years old, and I did not know how to swim, nor did I have any desire to go fishing. But he would not hear any argument from me. He had made arrangements for me to go commercial fishing for the summer as a bait boy on a trawler in order to learn a trade. The thought of my being with a stranger for a summer literally petrified me. I did not want to be away from my brother Butch, and I certainly did not want to go away with a man I did not know for three months. But at the insistence of my father, I took the bus ride from Seattle to Neah Bay the first Saturday after school was out. Arriving at the Makah Indian village of Neah Bay, after 10 hours on the bus, I was met by my boss, Red, who owned the commercial fishing boat "Far Away". It was a 32 foot trawler and Red was the only other person on the boat. It was midnight when I arrived in Neah Bay and very dark. Red put me in a rowboat and we rode out to where his fishing trawler was anchored. It was only then that I learned I was to be the only other person on the boat for the next three months! Those were the worst three months of my entire life. Red was an alcoholic and a very perverse individual who made my life a living hell aboard the boat. The next morning we headed out to the ocean where we spent two-week intervals fishing in fog banks out of sight of land. The trawler had four poles on each side, with each trailing lines of six baited hooks. The boat had one bunk, a small kerosene stove, and no radio or sonar. My job was to pilot the boat through the crowd of other boats while Red manned the eight trawler fishing lines. We would get up at 4 a.m. and fish until noon. My job was then to clean the fish after fixing breakfast of baked beans and toast or whatever undersized fish we happen to catch that day. In the afternoon Red began drinking gin and by nightfall, he was usually roaring drunk and abusive. There was no place to hide or to run from this man. If we needed supplies there was a supply barge at Swiftshure, 40 miles out in the ocean. It was there we sold our catch and restocked any necessary goods. When we went into port at the end of the first month, I looked for help, but there was no one I could trust. Most of the Indians kept to themselves, and there was no law enforcement to turn to. The other fishermen were very friendly with Red and clearly offered me no avenue of escape. I resigned myself to spending the summer doing the best I could to avoid the man whenever possible.

When I returned to Seattle in September I told my father I would not go fishing again. I had a severe stutter and was afraid of everyone. I was deeply ashamed of the things that happened. I could not get them out of my mind and I was afraid people would find out what he had done to me. I was ashamed I had not run away but where could I have gone?

The following summer my father told me I must go again to fish with Red. I told him some of the things that had happened the year before, and he said that I must not worry about it because there would be another man on the boat with us this year that he knew. I went back to Neah Bay, and that year, we fished in the Alaskan waters, as well as the ocean off Washington State. The other man, my father spoke of never materialized!

I remember piloting the boat and reading a small paperback book called "Microbe Hunters". It was about science and various discoveries throughout the years. I began to dream of someday graduating from school and doing something to help others. I was captivated by the importance of these inventors and their contribution to mankind in general. I remember specifically being impressed with Madame Curié and with Louis Pasteur. I began to find my escape in other books and I became an avid reader, escaping the daily/nightly torment by hiding in my own imagination. Red would tease me for hiding in books all the time but I read every book I could find! It helped me escape. When I returned to school in the fall, my speech was almost unintelligible and the school authorities put me in special classes to help.

My brother Butch was spending much of his time in the juvenile detention center for stealing cars, doing pot and drinking alcohol. He was rarely home, instead living with families of friends he made in school or in empty buildings or garages. I rarely saw him anymore. My brother Charles was now working for the US Coast and Geodetic Survey in Alaska, leaving me the only one still living at home with my mother and father.

It was ironic that most of the people at school were fascinated that I was a "commercial fishermen" in the summer months, and they wanted to know all about my "exciting" experiences. But I would simply tell them we went out fishing and it was very boring or I would ignore their questions.

The third summer came, and I was now 12 years old. My father said that I must go with Red once more, and this year Red had a new boat with a large crew. I told my father I would not go, but he insisted and when I refused he told me he was paid $100 each summer by Red for me to go fishing. He insisted there would be six people on the boat besides myself, and I would be perfectly safe. I trusted my father, and once more took the long bus ride to Neah Bay. Indeed, there was a new boat called the "Carrie A" and it had two other crew members besides me. Unfortunately, they turned out to be as addicted to alcohol and perversion as Red was. I found a friend in Cleon, a boy of my age whose father operated the ice plant. When we needed to buy ice for our catch in port I had to push the ice on to the long ramp that ran along the dock from the ice house to where we were moored. The ramp was about 10 feet high and when ice blocks got stuck my job was to climb up and dislodge them. Red so enjoyed my misery in this he loaned me to other boats when they bought ice! I took refuge in books, spending many quiet hours reading and escaping into my imagination, a tool that served me well in years to come.

I spent one last miserable summer commercial fishing on the West Coast to please my father. We traveled from Neah Bay to LaPush to Westport and up Vancouver Island to Skagway and Ketchikan, Alaska. The bigger boat was a comfort in that there were places to escape and some of the men tried to protect me from Red when he was drunk. When I returned in September, I told my father, I did not care what he did; I would never go with Red again. Ten years later I learned that Red went fishing off of Port Angeles in a rowboat with a friend and was lost at sea. I felt a great relief at the news.

## Chapter Four

# MY WORLD IMPLODES

*Job 16:1-5*

*16:1 Then Job answered and said,*
*2 I have heard many such things: miserable comforters*
*are ye all.*
*3 Shall vain words have an end? or what embold-*
*eneth thee that thou answerest?*
*4 I also could speak as ye do: if your soul were in my*
*soul's stead, I could heap up words against you,*
*and shake mine head at you.*
*5 But I would strengthen you with my mouth, and the*
*moving of my lips should assuage your grief.*
*KJV*

My fishing summers became my "breakaway event" from the family. The two older boys were now permanently gone from the home, and Butch was pretty much on his own living at his friend's homes or on the streets. Mother would turn to her books, drinking and work and my father spent his time when at home in his private workshop in the basement or working on cars in the backyard and garage. Rotating between several jobs, he was often away for two or three days at a time. I set up a card table in the dining room, which turned into my" desk" where I buried myself in school-work. I was painfully lonesome. I found my only joy and approval in getting good grades in school despite the ridicule I received from classmates for my appearance, stutters and lack of athletic ability. I found it hard to make friends because I could not bring people to the house, because I was embarrassed and because I did not know how much tension there would be whenever I got home. As our farm had become the suburbs with housing developments all around us, I earned money babysitting for neighbors and doing yard work with my objective to save enough money so that I could someday go to college. The fishing brought some savings, and I worked afternoons as a dishwasher in two restaurants. I was given a job in the high school library and at 14 years of age I was feeling good about myself, though socially awkward in oh so many ways. My one constant companion was loneliness. I did not have any close friends or anyone I could confide in. During the months on the fishing boat, I had learned to be alone and read to exercise my mind and fill time. My mantra was to trust no one and provide just for myself.

The neighbor girl whom I liked very much had invited me to her birthday party. At Christmas I bought her a giant candy cane which I carried home from Burien in a rainstorm. It took hours to repair the box from the water, wrap and present it as a gift. She was gracious when I gave it to her so the invite to a birthday celebration was great news. Excitedly, I took some of my savings and walked to Burien where I bought her a gift of a unicorn pin. Later, her mother phoned and told us the party was cancelled. I threw the pin away on her birthday, when I could hear the other kids playing at the party I had been uninvited to attend. I was heartbroken. Most of what neighbors we had wanted nothing to do with us and her parents were no exception. I withdrew from trying to be friends.

In the fall of 1953, things became weird at our house. One afternoon when I came home from school early, I found my father in one of the bedrooms drilling holes in the baseboard. It was a very tiny hole and was located in the corner where I would not have seen it if not catching him drilling. It seemed to me to serve no purpose. When asked what he was doing he got very angry with me, so I left, bewildered. Though our driveway entered on 169th street and the house faced a steep hill on 170th, we had a path from 170th street that we often came up. I began to notice small pieces of string laid across the path at waist height every day, from bush to bush in a zigzag pattern and was puzzled why anyone would do this and for what conceivable purpose. To get up the path from the street was a struggle for an adult and to put string across the path made no sense to me. There were pieces of string in windows and on door tops and a yellow yarn running around the outside walls of the entire house!

My dad had left his real estate business, selling insurance and teaching welding at night school, and was now working as a prison guard at the Washington State reformatory at Monroe. Because of the distance between our home and the reformatory, he did not come home as often, and his appearances came as a surprise. When he was home, he was clearly more angry and unsettled than before. One afternoon, I found him installing a speaker and microphone system in the wall of the living room. He said it was a joke for Christmas. He then placed a Santa Claus mask over the speaker and showed me he could talk through a microphone in the other room and have his voice come out from wall as "Santa Claus". It seemed bizarre to me because he had never shown any interest in Christmas or at levity, and it was simply out of character for him to play tricks or gags! But strange behavior was becoming commonplace and if I knew one thing for a certainty, it was dangerous to question dad!

In November he painted several light bulbs dark red and placed one in each room of the house. He told me the light bulbs were "infrared" and that they permitted him to take photos with his special camera through the walls into any room in the house which had a red bulb turned on. Every light fixture in the house was equipped with a "red bulb". I shrugged it off as another failed invention, never daring to question him.

For my 14th birthday, on December 12$^{th}$, my father made me a special bed in his workshop. It had an upholstered yellow striped headboard and was decorated with wood ornaments and attached to the wall in my upstairs room. I thought it an unusual present but it was something he made special for me and for that I was surprised and appreciative. It was one of just a few special things he had done for me, the other being a small wooden chair he made.

Then Christmas Eve, Butch had returned home for the holiday and we had decorated the house that day. Butch and I were called downstairs from our room about 10 o'clock at night. Dad and mom sat glaring at each other across the living room each seated on their own couch. It was clear they had been arguing violently. My father motioned for me to sit next to him on the couch and I did. Butch stood at the doorway, not wanting to come in the room. Dad spoke first, telling us the marriage was over. Mother tore off her wedding ring and threw it into the fire. Dad followed. My brother Butch ran out of the house and I was now alone with my two estranged parents. My dad produced a large manila envelope and said he didn't want to but he had to show me some photos. He pulled out 12 sheets and described each. The first, he said, was a picture of mother having sex with a boyfriend, "Bill the cab driver". Then one by one he described each as depicting her copulating with the dogs, with my brothers, the cab driver and even with me! He said we were not to blame because she had deceived us. Another was explained as a photo of "Bill the cab driver" crawling out the bedroom window. Pictures of oil drippings from the road below the house where "Bill the cab driver" would park his car and photos of strings pulled from the path showing someone had come up to the house by that "devious" route. It was horrible to hear and it was even harder to comprehend. The photos he was describing were all just blank pieces of paper! Clearly, he had "seen" these awful things in his mind! My mother just sat there stone-faced as he leveled the charges against her, and us. I sat at his side trying to understand with my 14 year-olds mind what was going on. When he finished ranting, he sent me back to bed, refusing to hear anything I tried to say. This was Christmas Eve! To this day, Christmas Eve is a very difficult time for me. Those scars never completely go away.

Christmas morning was not to be. The tree, decorations and gifts had been taken away during the night, and were heaped in the corner, presumably as punishment for whatever "we had done wrong" in not backing him. I just avoided seeing either of my parents for several days, staying in my room. We all walked on egg shells hoping not to cause any more outbursts or accusations, until at last my father returned to work at the reformatory. His habit was to leave Sunday evenings for the Reformatory which was 40 miles away, and return Tuesday and Friday evenings during the week. The other nights we believed he stayed in Monroe at the Institution, although now it was clear he was spying and trying to trap imaginary events on his cameras. He remained very cold and indifferent to me from that point on, uneasy and upset at my not being supportive. He clearly could not understand why I did not believe his "photo evidence".

I had no one to talk to or confide in. I did not trust the teachers at school, and I had no close associates or adults in my life that I could speak with. My father clearly was sick, and yet he was the anchor of my life and the one who provided my food, shelter, protection and everything. My parents had never been ones to give hugs or approval, but at least they had been strong people that I thought I could depend upon. Clearly they were not. Mother was totally involved in her alcohol escape and my father's mind had abandoned all sanity and reason.

In late January, another strange event occurred. Father came home on a Friday evening with blood on his clothes. He was driving a truck that belonged to his friend Dick Forsythe. When we asked about the blood, he said that he had been killing chickens, which did not make any sense, but his hostility caused us to not ask any further questions. It was a flatbed truck we recognized as it had been used for years by his friend, a junkyard sidekick. Dick collected junk and bargained in used stuff. He was a loner and had no family we knew of. Days later we learned the police were looking for Dick Forsythe when they came to the house asking if we had seen him. My dad said no, we had not. The sheriff asked why my father had his truck and dad said he had given it to him. The sheriff left and we heard nothing more.

A few days later, my father asked me to go with him to the store. Once in the car, we drove to the four acres property instead, and I remained in the car while my dad placed something in the well and then capped it off with concrete and gravel. I am convinced this was the final resting place for his friend. Later when I told the sheriff, they refused to believe me.

The weeks following, not much transpired around the house out of the ordinary. I kept cleaning the house and cooking after school. Dad would take mother to work and pick her up after, placing her in the bedroom. When he was away she took the bus to work and ate alone in her bedroom. She was growing more distant, as if she had given up on living.

Then came one Saturday evening when mom complained she could not sleep so dad gave her some sleeping pills. Later, he got very angry because she would not stay awake for his amorous intentions! He beat her severely and this time the marks showed about her head and face. I could hear the screaming from my room but when I came to help she sent me away! Dad just stood there glaring at her and me. It was awful because I knew what had happened but could do nothing about it. We just walked around the rest of the night like nothing had happened but no one willing to go to sleep. Clearly dad was now totally out of control and he knew it.

Fortunately, dad was so convinced mother was ill that he decided to take her to see a doctor the next day! I was relieved because I knew she needed medical attention. He was sure she was crazy and said so repeatedly.

He took her to a doctor in Seattle, a psychiatrist named Dr Stone. The professional immediately recognized that my dad was the one who was sick and told him he needed to speak with my mother privately "for analysis". While my father was waiting outside, he explained to my mother that dad's illness was extremely serious and dangerous and that he had to be institutionalized. He ordered commitment of my father to Western State Mental Hospital at Steilacoom, Washington. He said this would require several days to arrange and that the authorities would be out to pick up my father the coming Friday afternoon. She then returned to work, after the charade with dad being told by Dr Stone that mother was just overly tired and not ill. She then telephoned me at school and told me what the doctor had said. I truly didn't know what to believe. I was called out of class to the principal's office to receive a call from mother whom I barely knew. My father was literally the only parent and provider I had known, and yet he was pronounced crazy, dangerous and going to be put away. I didn't know what to think. My older brothers were all gone away. My kid brother

Butch was off and on living with friends. I had no one to talk to or turn to. It was my world crashing down on me. I recall going to the gym locker room after school and hiding in the showers and just crying my heart out. Moms said not tell anyone. I had no where to turn except to continue doing my chores and school work. As it was Wednesday, I went to the Alls' Well Restaurant where I worked afterschool and washed dishes. I arrived home at nine that night and went directly to bed. My father was not home. Mom was in the bedroom with her six pack of beer. Thursday night she wanted us to have Spaghetti Dinner as a special treat for dad as it was his favorite. When I got home Thursday dad was there and I could sense he knew something was wrong. Mom was more self-assured than usual and was preparing a big dinner and setting the dining room table and using the china! As I was going down the hallway, I looked into the kitchen and saw dad sprinkling a powder into the spaghetti sauce. I knew this was wrong as the container was a plain brown tin from his workshop. I didn't say anything but I knew I had to do something, when I was taking the sauce into the dinner table, I slipped and threw it on the floor. Mom just looked at me strangely like I had spoiled her special dinner. Dad came over and patted my shoulder saying it was okay. No words were said for the rest of the evening. Mom was angry with me for spoiling dinner and dad just wanted to be alone. I went to bed after doing the dishes. He went down into the basement and stayed the night in his workshop. This was his hiding place and forbidden territory to the rest of the family. To this day, I do not know what my father had added to the spaghetti sauce, but I believe it was not good.

Friday came and I biked to school as usual, not knowing what to expect. I washed dishes again at the restaurant after school and came home about 7, hoping all was okay. It was not. Around 7:30 six deputy sheriffs and a doctor arrived. Dad was in the basement. Mom was in her bedroom. I told a deputy where dad was and I was instructed to leave at once and stay far away from the house for an hour. I went up the hillside but when I looked back I saw my father on the front lawn being fought to the ground by all six men. He was finally subdued by the deputies and hauled away. Mother stayed in her room all night, came out the next morning and caught the bus to go to work, having overtime pay on Saturdays. Brother Butch came home Saturday afternoon and I told him what happened. He then told me that since Dad is crazy and I was his kid, I probably was crazy too, or would be. Thus developed the family slogan taken up by my brothers and even my mother "...your next", whenever I did anything wrong. That taunt haunted me for years. That I was his only kid was not so special anymore.

By Monday afternoon, the news had spread throughout the school of my father being taken to the mental hospital. I found notes on my locker, and on my desks in class. It was May and I only had the last six weeks before school was out. Because it was the ninth grade, next fall I would be in a new school. I found what few friends I had did no longer want to be around me. I could hardly wait for summer vacation.

The neighbors shut themselves away from us and no one came to offer any help whatsoever. I think they were afraid my dad would return. We received a petition signed by 83 people asking us to move. It was nailed to the front door when I came home from school. My mother kept it in her safety deposit box. Once in a while she would pull it out and look at it and then let loose some choice epithets. The day she died I burned it.

After two weeks, I asked mom if we could go visit dad at Steilacoom mental hospital. This was a considerable distance as it is about 45 miles away but we arranged it by bus. When we got there we went into the large day room. Dad looked awful. Now, I realize he was heavily sedated but at the time I had no such concept. He told me how horrible it was there.

He described the hot thermal bathes, electric shock treatments, and spinal taps. When I had to have a spinal tap years later at age 45 for medical reasons, I was still in great fear from his descriptions back when I was just 14 years old. He complained about the food, saying they fed him prunes and vegetables but not nearly enough meat or real food. In truth, he was severely overweight and for a certainty they were trying to have him lose weight. He weighed over 400 pounds most of his adult life. Finally, he asked my mother and the orderly if he could speak with me alone. I agreed it was okay and they let us talk in private.

While we were alone, dad said that they were trying to kill him and they were keeping his medicines from him. He said that in his black satchel case in the workshop at the house he had a package of a white powdered medicine he needed. He said they would not let him have it so I needed to secretly get it and bring it to him next time I came. He warned me not to tell mother or anyone else or they would tell the doctors! I was flustered but decided I would do as he said.

The following Saturday when mother caught the bus to work, I went to the basement. The outside windows had been painted over for years to keep anyone from looking in. This had been my dads refuge and retreat for years and no one else had been allowed in to his workshop. Having no key, I took a large hammer and tried to pry off the hasp on the door lock. It was too hard to get loose. I started hitting it with the hammer. Then I went and found a sledge hammer and flailed at the lock. Nothing! I got a 16 pound wrecking bar from the garage and struck at the door. It would not budge. I backed to the other side of the basement and ran at the door, hitting it with the pointed end of the wrecking bar. I began penetrating the door and splinters were flying in all directions, but still the lock would not budge. It was like the door had become a fabric of steel. I could see through parts of it into the dark room, but nothing clearly. No matter what I did, still I could not get the door open. At last, I hit on the idea of crawling in an outside window. I went out with the wrecking bar and dislodged a window casing and crawled in the room. Finally reaching the center through the maze of tools and equipment, I pulled on the string light and the room was illuminated. I was in total disbelief of what I saw. On the workbench were four webcore wire recorders, like today's tape recorders, each running continuously. On the ceiling were scores of small mirrors which were configured like periscopes, peeking into the upstairs bedrooms and closets. There were one-way mirrors looking up into the living room. Wires and tiny speakers dotted one large panel. A photo developing setup was arranged on another table,

But the thing that got my immediate attention was a shotgun strapped to the table saw placed directly in front of the door. It was attacked by string to the doorknob, and, it was loaded in spring gun fashion so that when the door was opened the gun would discharge chest-high! In shock and trembling, I ran upstairs and called the telephone exchange and asked them to call the sheriff. I could not grasp why my father would try to kill me but it was very clear he did! My very own father, the only person in the world I truly loved and trusted, had tried to shoot me with a shotgun!

told no one about the shotgun after it was removed by the sheriff, not even my mother. About a week later I decided I must see father and find out why. Reluctantly, mom agreed and we again took the bus trip to Steilacoom. When we arrived I was told I could not see dad. They said he had told them about the gun and he was under the belief he had succeeded in killing me and that for his treatment they thought it best for him to operate under the impression I was dead. I was angry and bewildered. The doctors said that he was glad he had killed me because I would never suffer the way he had and that he killed me out of love because as his only son, I would have eventually suffered the way he had. In his twisted thinking, his killing me was seen by him as a favor and act of compassion.

Going back to the house, I began to trace the wires from the Webcore recorders. For the most part, the microphone wires were just bunched up in the wall, spackled in place, and went nowhere. There is no possible way my father had been able to record anything, but in his head he had heard many hallucinations, apparently, for years. I found wires and small microphones on the walls of most rooms of the house, including in the headboard of the bed my father had made for me for my birthday. There were one-way mirrors, in many of the rooms and wires throughout the attic that lead nowhere. I removed the system of mirrors, and "periscope's" he had constructed and spackled over the holes in the bedrooms. All of the "red light bulbs" were destroyed and camera equipment sent to the dump.

I withdrew. I was through with people. I closed my mind to everyone and everything. At 14, I shut out the world! The only thing I trusted was what I learned for myself. I engaged myself at all times in reading, doing my school work, and doing my jobs. I continued at the restaurant washing dishes and I got another job at the library on Saturdays and three afternoons, and, I earned money cleaning three barbershops on Monday evenings. Brother Butch was now in juvenile detention or living with friends so mother and I lived alone. It was as if we were strangers in the big house. I cooked dinners and cleaned house as best I could. She went to work and came home by bus everyday, arriving at 6:40 promptly with her six pack of beer. By 8:00 each night she was sobbing "why, why why, God why me" and by 9:00 pm she usually passed out and I would put her to bed. I slept in the living room as we could not afford to heat the whole house. On cold days I burned some chairs, a chest of drawers, and an old big victrola cabinet, and stuffing from several old mattresses.

Under a tarp in the workshop I found an old bed and recalled it once was used by my father when he slept down in the basement away from the family. But as I thought about it I realized he slept there with me when I was younger. He use to say he needed to "watch me" because I had a bed wetting problem when I was five or six. But the more I reflected the more I recalled he did some unthinkable things to me that had little relationship to any "bed-wetting", and then I got angry! This became the first mattress I burned in the fireplace to heat the house.

Mother realized I was struggling and my stutter was getting much worse so she arranged for me to meet with the psychiatrist that committed dad. Dr Stone talked with me, explaining my father was a paranoid schizophrenic, probably a result of head injuries sustained when he was a boxer in his youth. He said as his only son, I had nothing to fear in being his son, and to help me be sure, he gave me some written tests. I took the papers and filled them out as best I could and then handed them to his receptionist. About fifteen minutes later, Dr Stone came out and told he had reviewed the tests, determined I was quite normal, and had nothing to be concerned out regarding my father and my eventual mental health. This sounded great except for one thing. My "tests" were still on the corner of the receptionists desk in plain sight and it was very clear to me the good doctor was lying to me, not having even looked at the tests. There went my faith in the medical profession right out the window. I was angry with him but more with my mother in trying to perpetrate such an obvious hoax! I decided for some curious reason I would not live beyond 27 years. It was a fixation with me to make the best used of the time I had but have no plans beyond the appointed time. At age 27, I became a new creation in Christ Jesus when He granted me the gifts of The Holy Spirit and my eyes were opened!

45

In July, our garage caught fire and burned to the ground. The fire was set by one of our neighbors, but no one who could prove who did it. We did not need the garage as we had no running vehicles anyhow, but the house power lines had been affixed to the garage roof. The power company said they would restore power to the house but we had to pay for a power pole and as it was on private property and only served our house, it would be at our expense of $94.00. No chance we had that kind of money. The state was taking $200 each paycheck from mom for fathers care at Steilacoom and we were heavily in debt everywhere. After five months, we reached "agreement" with Puget Sound Power to pay $5 each month, and the pole was installed and electricity restored. Years later the power company attached lines to four new houses to our pole and I complained until they removed them! Mother threatened to "totem" our pole with the faces of Puget Sound Power & Light officers' likenesses, until her dying day.

This episode plus moms increased crying through the nights, now drinking bourbon along with the nightly six-pack, and her hostility to everyone but me, led to a poor decision on my part. I decided to ask my two older brothers for help. I sat down and wrote Henry and Charles about the situation at home and asked both of them to seek a hard-ship discharge from the military and come home and help me. At 14, the episode with Puget Sound power showed me there were very few things I could do in running the home and mother was clearly in no condition to make good deci-sions. Though I had savings for college from my commercial fishing summers and from work, the bank would not let me have a checking account, meaning I had to run all over on my bike and the bus to pay bills. When I had to deal with the Power Company and fire department about the garage fire they would not even pay me any attention until they first tried to talk with mom. Since they could not get her attention, they finally talked with me and "let us get by" but it was embarrassing. I struggled all the time trying to keep things secret at school and elsewhere but it was talking a toll on me emotionally.

Brother Henry wrote me back from Okinawa where he was stationed in the Navy. He said he would not leave the military, that he did not believe me or mom that dad was "that sick" (he had been away about six years now) and that if things were tough at home I should run away and join the military like he did. He did not realize that at 14 years of age I could hardly join the Navy.

Brother Charles gave me hope! He was in the Air Force stationed at Lackland Air Force Base in San Antonio, Texas. He also expressed concern that dad was not "crazy" and he felt mother and I had plotted this incarceration! But, he said he had leave coming in October and he would come back to Seattle to see if he could help me and to evaluate the situation himself. He said he would be home October 27th. I was relieved that at least someone would help, though I didn't know my older brother very well. He was 10 years older and Henry was twelve years older. I counted the days until he would arrive. Then my hopes were dashed. It was about 2 AM on October 24thth. I was asleep in the living room when I could see a flashlight beam coming in the window and then pounding on the front door, I opened the door and was surprised to see a cab driver. Ironically, his named patch said "Bill"! All I could think of was there it is "Bill, the cab driver" just as my dad had said. For a brief second I was filled with doubts and fear. Then he spoke and it was clear her had never been here before and did not know us.

He was hostile, having just found the house by coming up the path through the brush from the roadway below, rather than on the driveway which entered from the back-street to our house. Our driveway was at the back of the house on 169th street and the front was woods and brush though the house number was to 170th street. I came to my senses quickly and realized he was asking for Alice Riess. I said she was asleep and he said he had a black border telegram for her about her son Charles. Charles had been killed in a car accident that morning in San Antonio, Texas. He would not be coming home. I woke mother and told her and asked her what we should do. The telegram said an Air Force representative would be contacting us to make arrangements within 24 hours. I asked mom what we should do and she replied with advice I have kept to this day. She said you just put one foot in front of the other and keep doing what you need to do. Her job was to go to work and mine was to go to school. So, that is what we did. I was now alone for a certainty. I took the telegram from him, put it on the mantle, and cried myself to sleep. Charles was the only brother, who ever tried to look out for me, even though he clearly did not believe that dad was sick when he was hospitalized. It grieves me that all three of my brothers were gone when the defining events occurred resulting in dads' commitment. Though brother Butch was still home occasionally, he was so involved in marijuana and alcohol that he barely noticed what was going on in the family home. Years later, Butch also confided in me that the two older boys were incensed that mother bought me my law school education and paid for my law office with whatever "wealth" they imagined that she had taken from putting dad away. It broke my heart to hear these falsehoods, but also explained why the brothers had resented me so much through the adult years.

# Chapter 5

# ENTERING THE WORLD

*Isa 49:9-16*

*9 That thou mayest say to the prisoners, Go forth; to them that are in darkness, Shew yourselves. They shall feed in the ways, and their pastures shall be in all high places.*

*10 They shall not hunger nor thirst; neither shall the heat nor sun smite them: for he that hath mercy on them shall lead them, even by the springs of water shall he guide them.*

*11 And I will make all my mountains a way, and my highways shall be exalted.*

*12 Behold, these shall come from far: and, lo, these from the north and from the west; and these from the land of Sinim.*

*13 Sing, O heavens; and be joyful, O earth; and break forth into singing, O mountains: for the Lord hath comforted his people, and will have mercy upon his afflicted.*

*14 But Zion said, The Lord hath forsaken me, and my Lord hath forgotten me.*

*15 Can a woman forget her sucking child, that she
should not have compassion on the son of her
womb? yea, they may forget, yet will I not forget
thee.*
*16 Behold, I have graven thee upon the palms of my
hands; thy walls are continually before me.*
*KJV*

Mother divorced my dad on grounds of mental cruelty
the following year in order to cease our obligation for his monthly $240.00 medical expenses in the state
hospital. The following winter, the old oil furnace gave out.
Washington State demanded back property taxes on our home
and the four acres property which my father had neglected to
pay for three years. We had no choice but to use my college
funds from fishing, and my various jobs. So, at 15, I became
the caretaker of the home though it was in my mothers name
from the divorce. She promised it would be deeded to me
when she died, unless she was able to pay back the money
sooner. My three brothers all had put nothing into keeping
the house. Later, in 1969, I purchased a home for her in Las
Vegas and she deeded the Gregory Heights home to me for
an additional $10,000.00.

By now, the school authorities realized I was becoming
a basket case. My schoolwork was incredibly good, I was
always punctual, but my clothes were a mess, I would not
associate with any other students, and when cornered and
required to answer to anything in class or outside, my stutter
made it very difficult to comprehend what I was saying. They
had a speech therapist see me at school for two afternoons
each week. I received speech training and was enrolled in
debate class. I took to debate very well; it was a natural fit.
Though I did not like to associate with others because I was
afraid they would penetrate my heart and find out about my
home life and cause more hurt, I did love debating and became

very good at it. This led to an interest in law, several college scholarships and grants, and a way out of my personal hell. By my junior year in high school I won several tournaments including college competitions in oratory, extemporaneous speaking, Student congress, and cross-question debate.

Because bus service was inadequate in the Gregory Heights house, mother bought a car, an old Chevrolet Coupe. Without the garage in the back, we needed some help in removing the debris and putting in a new one or a new driveway. Someone referred a builder to mother and he was willing to put in a garage, stairway and drive in the front yard of the house in exchange for the three other lots, our back yard lot which faced 169th street, and the four acres. This seemed a very high price because we were giving four building lots away. After much negotiation, it was agreed between mother, myself and the builder that he would place a 2 car garage in front, put in concrete driveway and stair-case, grant a fenced 10 foot right-of-way in the back so we would retain some of the fruit trees and a level entry to the house for delivery of large items, and, he would put in a full rockery and would pay me and train me in doing the work. Actually, he never gave us any easement. He fenced off the back, put in a single car garage and asphalt drive, and had the rocks delivered. I got paid nothing for my work. I did learn to construct a rockery and I now was more than ever interested in becoming a lawyer! That he took advantage of us, knowing what we had already been through, was one of the more influential events in my young life causing me to distrust others and wanting to go into law for protection. He caused us a great deal of hurt when we were vulnerable. Mother was too emotionally whipped to fight back and at 15 I could hardly carry the battle. Mom had signed the papers trusting in what he promised and that was that.

No longer spending evenings away in her bedroom, mother would "nest" on the couch in the living room with her six-pack, a bottle of Four Roses bourbon, and her Pall Malls each evening. Relieved of the violent outbursts and unpredictable behavior of dad, she had few parenting skills in her new role as head of the house. Acquiring a Zenith television set, she resorted to tossing darts at us if we strolled in front of the screen. Butch was nailed squarely in the butt one evening when visiting us, a moment he did not soon forget or forgive! But each evening she continued to drink herself to sleep, crying out "why, oh god, why?" as she drifted off. I had no answers for her. For my 16th birthday she wanted to "buy me a hooker" as though that would resolve any lingering questions I might have about the mystery of sex. I was incensed at the very thought and angry she found this the best substitute for parenting. My rigid moral code would not permit such behavior and probably because of the affront I felt, I remained celibate until my wedding night!

Brother Butch ran off to Idaho with his girlfriend and married at age 17 and had two kids. He had been living with her in her parents' basement off and on since she became pregnant so their elopement seemed inevitable. He worked pumping gas at a local gas station and I would see him on occasion but we had drifted far apart in our own worlds. While I was totally inward and fending off all efforts of others to invade my world, he was experimenting with everything imaginable trying to find pleasure, peace and fulfillment in every destructive way he could.

Two teachers asked that I not come to the bacculerate service at graduation, probably because of my clothes and general appearance, and possibly because they thought my mother would show up as well. I obliged, but it hurt. Mother did manage to show for my high school graduation, but she was inebriated and I would have preferred her not being there. We had been through a lot together and she viewed us as "buddies" though I had resented her drinking, her swearing, and her bitterness. It was very embarrassing for me to take her anywhere, because she kept repeating the same stories over and over. She obviously was obsessed, and a dysfunctional alcoholic. She refused help, making it uncomfortable for me to be around her. The sudden outbursts, her passing out, and the slurs and racisms she reveled in left me cold and indifferent. We were forced together for the last four years, but I was looking forward only to getting away from home and on with my own life. I simply preferred to be left alone, working on the house or putting in the yard or doing my schoolwork. She would bring me a six-pack of root beer and a Chunky bar along with her beer and bourbon, thinking we were comrades. It is amazing she was not arrested for DUI all those years. I could not wait to get away and yet everyone who saw us thought of us as so close and such good friends. When on my 16th birthday she brought home a "lady" for me, thinking this was the best way to give me a "sex education", I made up my mind to just get through high school and then leave. For all my faults and transgressions, I was basically a square person. I knew you could not buy "love or affection" and a prostitute was hardly a replacement for good parental advice! I ran off for the evening and slept in the car. She upped the ante for my 21st birthday, giving me a membership in Playboy Clubs and their magazine subscription. Bless her for trying in her own way.

One Saturday night she became violent about something and I had no idea what was going through her mind. Trying to reason with her, she grabbed a Samari Sword that hung on the wall as a decoration and cut me across the stomach! The sword was a WWII souvenir we had had for years. The cut was not deep but served to make me more cautious about keeping such things around the house and to realize how detached her mind was when drinking. Bazaar behavior I expected but now I took note of the attendant danger posed as well. In the years past she had kept snakes and lizards as pets and even an alligator she named George. The alligator was the result of a television show, "Short Comings With Al Cummings". Al Cummings was a radio Deejay who advanced to television talk show. One afternoon he appeared on the show with an alligator someone had sent him from the South. He was seeking a new home for the alligator as it was sick and he did not know how to care for it. Mother grabbed the phone and was rewarded by her effort, the alligator was hers for the asking. We drove to Lake City to pick it up. Her erratic driving got the attention of a Seattle Policeman and she was pulled over. She convinced him she could still drive but after the explanation of where we were going and very brief physical testing, we were allowed to continue only if I drove! Fetching the alligator, about 8 inches long, we brought it home and proceeded to give it baths in milk and mineral oil and to hand feed it raw hamburger. She housed it in a big bakers pan on the fireplace hearth but after a few years I convinced her to donate it to the Woodland Park Zoo.

By my senior year in high school I needed better income than the part time jobs I had strung together. I was hired by Ford Motor at their parts depot in Seattle as a janitor for the summer months. Working with an African-American gentleman, I enjoyed his companionship on the job and was bewildered by all the hatred I had heard for years. Three weeks later I was promoted to unloading freight car loads of car parts at the parts warehouse. I earned very good money and I began to get excited about the prospect of leaving all behind for college. From my debate tournament experiences at local colleges and universities I gleaned a lot of information on where to go for a good strong college and pre-law educa-tion. I narrowed my choices to just three, College of Puget Sound, situated in Tacoma, Lewis & Clark in Portland, and Whitman College of Walla Walla, in Eastern Washington. All had good faculty and programs though Whitman clearly was my preference, and by far the most expensive. I decided the Tacoma school was too close to home, and Lewis & Clark in Portland was near where my mothers' father lived, so at the last minute I ruled both of those out and I applied only to Whitman College in Walla Walla. In May, I was notified that my financial statement was such that there was no way the admissions board believed I could afford the school and denied my application to Whitman. My grades were good and the scholarships and grants would be honored, but I would not be able to carry the outside jobs I contemplated and still have sufficient time for studies. I wrote back and told them I was not applying elsewhere and that I was certain I would succeed if they only gave me a chance. The board of admissions reconsidered and in July notified me that I was granted admission to Whitman College starting in the fall, on a trial basis.

By telephone, I told mother I had been accepted to Whitman in Walla Walla, and would be moving there in September. She said that was wonderful. She knew of Whitman because she had lived at St Paul's Episcopal Boarding School in Walla Walla for her 6th through 12th grades when her parents lived in Butte, Montana. She said she would apply for a transfer of her job from Seattle General Services Administration (GS-5) to Army Corps of Engineers in Walla Walla, sell the house and we would move there together I said no. I told her it was time for me to leave home and I was going alone. I told her I had taken care of her long enough and it was time for me to look after myself. She beat me to it! She left home! She came home from work, packed her bags, got into her car on Friday night, and drove away without a word. It was about a week before I realized she was not coming back! Six weeks later I found she had moved to Albuquerque, which was fine with me. It was a relief to no longer have to worry about her falling asleep on the couch with a lighted cigarette in hand, driving off the road, or passing out in public. I kept working at Ford Motor and taking care of the house as best I could that summer.

In September I enrolled at Whitman College, obtaining jobs at the College infirmary at midday (which gave me a free lunch), working as a server in the dining hall each evening, doing research in the College library, and cooking at a local restaurant, Pete's' Charcoal Broiler. I succeeded in keeping my grades up, avoiding fraternities and social functions, and making a few friends of independent campus types. Whitman was a good choice scholastically but I found I resented the opulent lifestyle and wealth of many classmates. Their fancy cars, ski weekends and summer vacations left me uncomfortable. I felt I was not welcome in their world, which helped me devote my attention to studies and work. But mostly, I resented the drinking and alcohol abuse, having been caregiver to my mother the last four years and now seeing my brother Butch going down the same shallow path.

I rented out the home in Gregory Heights and applied the proceeds to its upkeep, back taxes and my school expenses. I was scared to death that I would fail in my first semester in college. All of my life I have been told that I was stupid and incapable of learning. I had made it through high school by applying myself and concentrating on trying to figure out the answers that teachers wanted. College was a whole different ballgame, and I was in great fear. I had no choice but to succeed. There were no other options for me. If I failed, I would lose my scholarships and grants and not be able to continue on in college. There was no safety net. No alternate plan. It was all or nothing.

I decided the best route was to saturate myself with as much learning in my classes as possible. That way when it came time for tests I would have the best possibility of passing. I got five tablets, one for each class. I took four bottles of ink in different colors and quill type pens and set them on the counter. When I came home from class, I would outline the lecture for each subject in the notebook, alternating the color of ink. Then I would do the reading for the course and again outline in the notebook. Then I would read my notes back into a tape recorder and play it over and over until I had memorized the course material. This took a great deal of time, but it served me well in learning the material in school. I knew that others thought of me as unsociable. But I had little choice and was more comfortable staying to myself than interacting with others. They had money for activities and weekends. I had very little to spare for anything, bringing home leftovers from the infirmary and the restaurant for my meals. The results were that my grades were very good. And I had little difficulty keeping my scholarship and grants status.

Years later, at the 40th class reunion, I was incensed to hear classmates tell how in their fraternities they had the test questions in advance, in some cases even sneaking into the faculty offices to steal the exams. One classmate in particular told how he pried open the windows of the faculty office and climbed in to get the tests for his fraternity and then sold them to three others. As they laughed about these experiences I couldn't help think how sad it was the rich and wealthy felt it was okay to cheat their way through school, while others struggled to do it the right way. I became livid inside as they joked and laughed, not caring how hard it had been for some of us to make it through or the unfairness of their behavior. I left the reunion weekend that night, not wanting to even spend another day with these people who cared so little about honor and character.

The freshman year went by fast and for that summer I got a job in Las Vegas, Nevada. A friend of my mothers from Seattle had moved to Las Vegas and recently underwent a divorce. He had a large house he needed to share with someone in order to meet expenses. He got me a job working for the Department of Energy. I collected air specimens and filters from test monitoring equipment located in several states all over the Southwest, following nuclear energy tests at Los Alamos base. The samples were brought back to Las Vegas and delivered by me to the UNLV testing lab, where radiation and other data were collected. This was a wonderful job for me, as it involved camping and traveling all around seeing the southwest states and visiting various areas I would not have been able to see otherwise. Between the test events, I worked in warehousing of supplies, delivering them to the test sites, and the University of Las Vegas campus, where the AEC conducted their test results. I was given a 4 wheel drive truck to drive, the freedom of visiting seven southwest states and numerous Indian reservations, and was paid for my time! It was like a vacation for me. The truck had radio command and my destination was often changed while I was on the road, making the job a big adventure!

Often, my roommate Larry would go with me on my trips. He loved to visit the various Indian reservations, where he had many friends and vast knowledge, having been with the Bureau of Indian affairs for several years. He taught me a great deal about Navajo and Hopi Indian culture and introduced me to many new friends in Arizona and New Mexico. One of my favorite events was to visit the Hopi Indian Reservation and learn of the Kachina ethnicity. This seemed safe for me, because they rarely asked questions about my life and were most unlikely to be involved in my activities following the brief summer job. Larry was just getting over his divorce so we both needed to have fun. I turned 21 while living with him in Las Vegas. My frugality complemented our household well as Larry had difficulty with the temptation to gamble away paycheck after paycheck. He had no children or major financial responsibilities but the gambling fever kept him broke most of the time. On the other hand, I had learned by necessity to budget and to only buy that which I really needed. I had no problem allocating $20 to a night of fun at a casino, or movie or night out but once the

$20 was gone I would gladly be content to go back home. For Larry, it was difficult to leave until he had spent every penny he could in trying to chase his losses, knowing "that the big win was just another slot machine away."

In the fall, I returned for my sophomore year at Whitman, my "breakaway year". My campus jobs continued and my grades became such that law school was becoming not just a dream but a realistic goal. I now had a job on weekends as a grill cook at the Marcus Whitman Hotel. The tenants in my home in Burien fell on hard times and had to return the house to me. I wrote off the last 6 months of overdue rent because their family breadwinner had suffered a stroke. They were grateful and left without any problem. Then my brother Butch, now in his second marriage, moved in to the Gregory Heights house at a low rent. I did not realize when I made the agreement with him that he was now a severe alcoholic and that I would never see a penny of rent from him. To make matters worse, he neglected the house and its contents. When I returned to Seattle, I found the front door on the front lawn, the piano exposed to the elements in a room with broken windows, and the laundry chute filled with beer bottles from the third floor to the basement. It was a hard blow to have my own brother treat me this way but a learning experience about addicts and their promises. Yet, I understood it was a product of his alcohol, so I let it go and set about repairing the house during the summer. He just disappeared on me! I got a job with Boeing aircraft working on the Bomarc II system as a matériel officer. My assigned purchasing client was Thiokol Corporation of Utah. They provided propellants for the rockets, among other things. I enjoyed working at Boeing and even considered returning once I had my law degree in later years.

My junior year at Whitman College I concentrated on my major of political science and I worked closely with the four professors assigned to that discipline. Enjoying a small apartment off-campus, I continued doing my work in the infirmary and college library and serving meals in the freshman dormitory for income. On weekends, I again had jobs as a short order cook in two restaurants. Knowing that law school was coming, I began looking at the enrollment requirements and financial needs, hoping upon hope I could continue pursuing a career in law. The dream seemed unlikely to be realized as I counted the cost and reviewed my resources.

About the same time, I sensed that someone was watching me. On several occasions I found an intruder had been in my apartment. I could find nothing missing, but my notes had been disturbed and inexplicably items had been moved around. On one occasion, I found a can of Copenhagen snuff on my desk. This was disturbing to me because my father had always chewed Copenhagen snuff and I knew no one else who used it. I could not understand why a container would appear on my desk. I thought my father still believed that I was dead, and he was transferred to a mental hospital in California two years before at the request of his parents, according to Steilacoom state hospital authorities.

I applied to return to work at Ford Motor Company for the summer at the end of my junior year and was told I was welcomed there. Returning to Seattle in June, I received a telephone call from the office of the US congresswoman Catherine May. She advised that I had been selected to serve as a legislative intern in her office for the summer in Washington, DC. My professors at Whitman College had made the application on my behalf, without telling me. I would be paid for my services as an intern and if I accepted I was required to report to her office within one week. I notified Ford Motor Company that I would not be working for them. I packed my belongings in my 1946 Volkswagen Beetle and headed from Seattle to Washington, DC. I bought the Volkswagen for $200 from a service man who brought it back from Europe after graduation from high school. It had a split rear window, and hand operated turn signals that came out from the post behind the driver's door as a wooden paddle with two yellow reflector lights. When you pulled a rope located above the drivers' door, the paddle would stick straight out for a left turn, or, pulling harder, it would stick straight up indicating a right turn! I was not sure the old car would make it clear across the country. But I saw no other choice but to try. Here I was at age 22 driving across the entire continent in an old VW beetle with a sleeping bag and my two changes of clothing. What an exciting adventure I had. I slept in my car and bought loaves of cheese and bread for sandwiches for my meals along the way. I could not believe my good fortune to have been treated so well by my professors and to have received this exciting opportunity not only to see the country but to learn about our history and legislative process. In Nebraska, I fell asleep and drove into a cornfield but caused no major damage to the car. In St. Louis, I decided to stop at a motel and spend the money for a room for the evening. I stopped at a small motel on the outskirts of town but the manager told me it was closed. It was their last night in their apartment as they were going to tear down the building the next day. I explained why I was traveling and he and his wife invited me not only to stay in the motel for free, but had me join them for their farewell dinner as well! It appears someone was clearly looking after me. Driving on turnpike toll roads so common in the East for the first time in my life, I arrived in Washington, DC on Friday afternoon, about 3 p.m. It was awesome. In five days I had driven from Seattle to the nation's capital across the entire USA. Just seeing the monuments in Washington D.C. opened my eyes to so much history.

With the help of strangers, I was able to locate the office of Congresswoman Catherine May, a third term representative from Eastern Washington State. Her administrative assistant, John Knievel, took me into her private office where I was greeted by her most graciously. She handed me a manila envelope and asked me to take it with Mr. Knievel to the White House. I hopped into my little Volkswagen car with John Knievel and we drove up Pennsylvania Avenue to the White House, where we were admitted at the gate by a grinning Marine and where I parked my car next to several limousines in front of the White House west portico. Two Marines then escorted us into the oval office, where I met President John F. Kennedy and handed him the manila envelope. He was very cordial, and we spoke with him for about 20 minutes as I gave him the papers from Congresswoman May. Obviously, this meeting had been prearranged by her, and I was one star-struck kid from the boondocks feeling that I was way over my head!

The entire summer under the tutelage of Congresswoman May was like a dream come true. I shared a small apartment with a legislative intern from Maine, who was working for Senator Edmund Muskie. His assignment, as well as those of most of my 18 counterpart interns, was to run errands or send out booklets or form letters to constituents. Mrs. May had me crafting legislation, interpreting legislation, attending congressional hearings with her, and visiting many federal agencies. Since she did not drive, she assigned her special yellow congressional license plate to my Volkswagen. This resulted in my being able to park my beetle anywhere in the district and to be waved through all intersections that were manned by the District traffic police. She provided me with her private tickets to embassy events, State Department hearings, the Fourth of July fireworks celebration at the foot of the Washington Monument, and similar special occasions. Knowing that I was a fan of Senator Barry Goldwater, she arranged for me to sit next to him on several occasions at dinners and breakfast meetings. Since Congresswoman May Was Head of the House Agriculture Committee, she was influential in circles of power. She was the only woman invited to dine at the special Lyndon Baines Johnson table in the Congressional cafeteria. This was a large round table set aside by the House speaker for his invitees where much of the real legislative horse-trading went on. As a consequence, she had me join her for lunch on several occasions, exposing me to many of the most influential people in Congress. Washington State Senator Henry "Scoop" Jackson permitted me to serve two weeks in his office so that I was exposed to Senate procedures during my internship. Under his tutelage, I was allowed to visit the Senate floor and the Senate chambers while proceedings were in recess. I felt very privileged, and blessed during this summer of 1961. Yet for all of the ceremonial events, and unique opportunities I was granted, few people realized the inner fear and apprehension I was experiencing. I suffered continuing nightmares that somehow someone would expose my past, and I would be ashamed and humiliated. Because of this, I did little outside of the office and the Congressional responsibilities other than visiting many of the museums, historical sites and Civil War battlefields, on my own. I attended concerts and plays but made no lasting friends. I was much afraid something would take all this away and I would be humiliated.

In October, I returned to Whitman College for my senior year. I wrote columns for the college newspaper detailing my experiences in Washington, DC, and I made application to return to our nation's capital as a law student at George Washington University, at the invitation and encouragement of Congresswoman Catherine May and her staff.

Upon graduation from Whitman, I was accepted at the George Washington University Law School, John Foster Dulles National Law Center, and was granted scholarship through the Scottish Right Foundation, Republican National Committee, and several other fine organizations. My dream had come true. I was going to law school! Other than my mother graduating from high school, I was the first one in our entire family, to my knowledge, who completed anything above a GED high school equivalent degree.

A Psalm of David.

**138** I will praise thee with my whole heart: before the gods will I sing praise unto thee.

² I will worship toward thy holy temple, and praise thy name for thy lovingkindness and for thy truth: for thou hast magnified thy word above all thy name.

³ In the day when I cried thou answeredst me, and strengthenedst me with strength in my soul.

⁴ All the kings of the earth shall praise thee, O LORD, when they hear the words of thy mouth.

⁵ Yea, they shall sing in the ways of the LORD: for great is the glory of the LORD.

⁶ Though the LORD be high, yet hath he respect unto the lowly: but the proud he knoweth afar off.

⁷ Though I walk in the midst of trouble, thou wilt revive me: thou shalt stretch forth thine hand against the wrath of mine enemies, and thy right hand shall save me.

⁸ The LORD will perfect that which concerneth me: thy mercy, O LORD, endureth for ever: forsake not the works of thine own hands.

T

KJV

# Chapter Six

# JURISPRUDENT ADVENTURES

*2 Kings 4:2-7*

*2 And Elisha said unto her, What shall I do for thee? tell me, what hast thou in the house? And she said, Thine handmaid hath not any thing in the house, save a pot of oil.*

*3. Then he said, Go, borrow thee vessels abroad of all thy neighbours, even empty vessels; borrow not a few.*

*4 And when thou art come in, thou shalt shut the door upon thee and upon thy sons, and shalt pour out into all those vessels, and thou shalt set aside that which is full.*

*5 So she went from him, and shut the door upon her and upon her sons, who brought the vessels to her; and she poured out.*

*6 And it came to pass, when the vessels were full, that she said unto her son, Bring me yet a vessel. And he said unto her, There is not a vessel more. And the oil stayed.*

*7 Then she came and told the man of God. And he
said, Go, sell the oil, and pay thy debt, and live
thou and thy children of the rest.
KJV*

The summer of 1961, I decided to live for three months
with my mother in Albuquerque, New Mexico, where I
obtained employment as a day laborer with Ernie Ashcraft
homes. I figured I could handle it for the brief summer; it had
been four years since we had been together for any length
of time and mother was not drinking as severely. She now
worked once again For the General Services Administration
in order to complete the 30 years of service necessary for her
retirement benefits. We got a long well that summer, and it
was a good experience to be treated by her as an adult and
not as caregiver.

In September, I headed back to Washington, DC,
to begin my law school career at George Washington
University. When I arrived, I was welcomed back into the
staff of Congresswoman Catherine May and was permitted
to work whatever free hours I had on an hourly basis so as
not to interfere with my law school classes. The university
required as an incoming student to their University that I
live in the campus dormitory. But as an upperclassman, they
categorize me as a resident "monitor" in charge of super-
vising 16 incoming freshmen. I immediately moved out, not
wishing to be entangled as a dorm mother with all of the
additional responsibility of law school. This resulted in an
ongoing dispute between me and the finance office. I won.
Two years later they finally wrote off the "unpaid dorm fees.
Providentially for me, a member of Congresswoman Mays'
staff was leaving on an extended trip, leaving their apartment
available for my use. Unfortunately, the Park Hotel would not
permit the sub-letting of his apartment. As a consequence, I
was reduced to sneaking in and out of the building with my

belongings when I moved from the dormitory and for the succeeding six months that I lived there. This added a sense of adventure to the entire law school experience. The university was searching for me to pay room rent and insist I work as dorm mother, and, the hotel had no idea I was living there. Each day became a new adventure as I found novel ways to avoid the doorman.

I commenced my classes in law school with the same apprehension as I did in college. With my trusted notebooks, quill pens, and a tape recorder in hand, I was again convinced I would fail out of school at the earliest opportunity. This fear served me well as my grades continued to move me on towards graduation. Congresswoman May was helpful in seeing to it that I had use of the offices not only of her bureau but that of other federal agency libraries, as I pursued my degree in jurisprudence. I did research in Libraries of the Department of Commerce, Justice Department, Office of Housing and Urban Affairs, and Department of Agriculture! After six months it became necessary for me to find new lodgings, and I located the ideal situation for me at 17th & "R" Street Northwest. In this decidedly African-American neighborhood, I took a basement apartment in the Roxborough, at a reduced room rate, because I served as custodian part time. My job was to mop the tile floors on each six levels, take out the garbage, keep the lobby appearance up, and to tend the furnace at night. For this, I paid $200/ month for a $550 apartment. The law school was 29 blocks away, but the walking time was helpful in improving my memorization skills and keeping me healthy. For extra income, I worked with the Washington, DC public defender's office as an intern, bringing in additional funds for my law books. On weekends, I spent much time in the Smithsonian Institute, and I continued to attend the free outdoor concerts at Watergate (A park with barge-stage on the Potomac River at that time) and Sylvan theater (Located at the base of the Washington

Monument) presentations of Shakespeare in the Park, for entertainment. I continued on in summer school and took additional courses at the Catholic law school, Georgetown University, in order to achieve as many credits towards graduation as rapidly as possible.

Still, the cloud of my past hung heavy on me as I avoided friendships and close associations with anyone. Sometimes I would be extremely lonely and I would go to the movies and sit in the back row. Observing what appeared to be families in the theater, I imagined I was part of them and enjoyed the movie all the more with this fantasy. However, if they noticed me I would immediately leave the theater. On some occasions, I was lonely enough that I would go to a bar or tavern and order 7-Up and pretended I was with other people who appeared to be having a good time. In truth, I was painfully shy and very concerned that anyone would bring me to a sense of shame. It is ironic that political people were grooming me with an intent that I would become a politician or a public official when in fact, what I craved was a private life without social commitment. Deep down, I mis-trusted everyone and I suspected the worst of all who came across my path. Because of violence in my neighborhood, I befriended one very big African American man who lived on the streets near my apartment. He kept his meager belongings beneath the wood steps of a Laundromat near 16th and "R" street and often begged money for booze. He had cuts and bruises and clearly lots of street presence. One day he approached me for money. I gave him fifty-cents, showing him it was all I had with me. I explained I was a student and just didn't have much. From then on, he treated me as a friend and warned others not to do me any harm! If others asked me for money I would simply say "I gave my money to Jake and when he pays me back you can use it". They would leave me alone from then on. I didn't mind living in the black neighborhood as most were kind to me and presented no problems for me.

At the local stores, in particular the Payless Drug at DuPont Circle, some clerks resented me and served everyone else making me wait at the end of the line, but I didn't mind as I understood their resentment from their past hurts.

When I entered my final year of law school I found that I had sufficient credits to graduate, but only lacked residency requirements. To fulfill this, I enrolled in a moot Court class as my only course in my senior year. I was assigned a case involving theft of a fur coat. The third week, I won my case on a Summary Judgment Motion (legal argument on a point of law). My professor signed off as fulfilling the requirements of the course and I left for Seattle having completed all law school requirements in just over two years. My degrees of LLB Bachelor of Law, and Jurist Doctorate of Law arrived in Seattle by mail the following June. By then, I was already working for the law firm of Schweppe, Ritter, Doolittle, and Krug, the most prestigious constitutional law firm in Seattle. I was 25 years old in 1965, living in the old Gregory Heights house and working in arguably the most prominent law firm in Seattle. Several Firms had interviewed me in Washington D.C plus Boeing Company but I selected the Schweppe Firm because of its reputation and incomparable law library. Alfred Schweppe was a legend in Seattle, the former Dean of the University Of Washington School Of Law and arguably one of the best constitutional law practitioners west of the Mississippi River, if not the Country.

The case load I handled at the Schweppe firm was fascinating. One of my first assignments was to represent clients interested in repealing the Washington State "blue laws", laws prohibiting sales of certain items on Sundays. Their desire was to draw as much public attention and awareness to these outdated laws as possible in support of a public initiative, scheduled for the ballot in the general election in November to repeal the laws. A quirky Seattle lawyer who loved the controversy was one of my clients.

He would go into a store on Sunday and purchase peanut butter or Metrical diet beverage or even just a newspaper, accompanied by members of the press. He would then have me bring suit against the county prosecutor, demanding in a writ of mandamus that he prosecute the store for violating the "blue laws" by selling on Sundays. In fact, the laws were mostly ignored by everyone but our clients wanted them off the books. Another client was a Mount Vernon automobile dealer who had me bring suit against the prosecutor's office in Mount Vernon for a declaratory judgment that the laws were "moot". These cases were lots of fun for a new lawyer. Others were religious organizations that observed Saturday as the Sabbath, and, clients whose stores simply wished to operate on Sundays. Our clients were very satisfied, as the cases moved into public view, causing great support for repeal of the blue laws. The initiative passed overwhelmingly the following November. By that time, I had made three arguments before the state Supreme Court against various prosecutors, quite a feat for an attorney of just 7 months.

Another case I was assigned involved representing homeowners, aggrieved by the condemnation of their properties to make room for expansion of a freeway system known as the Thompson Expressway. We found irregularities in the procedures taken by the state in their proceedings against the homeowners and managed to thwart the efforts of the state and render their plans unworkable. The result of this was interruption of construction of the interstate freeway system in Seattle. We ended up with numerous spurs and on and off ramps that were simply suspended in mid air and unable to connect to the contemplated Thompson Expressway, now blocked by the court due to wrongful condemnation procedures. The connecting freeways had to be abandoned. The concrete spurs dotted the interstate system for years before the gurus of the highway department found ways to employ them in alternate manners, and the Thompson Expressway was never completed. Years later, the same homeowners were displaced by yet another freeway construction but given proper notice, hearing opportunity and compensation.

I enjoyed my years at Schweppe, Ritter, Doolittle and Krug and it gave me great exposure before the superior court and appeals court system early in my career. My work was supervised by knowledgeable and talented senior lawyers who did as much for my law career as years of schooling! My cases were in assisting others as only partners had full responsibility for any case. As the junior man I had exposure to the crème de'la crème litigation in the North West of the United States! Then the day came when the firm needed for me to buy in as a partner or move on to new fields. For me to buy in would have required nearly a half million dollars, and my net worth, apart from the Gregory Heights house to which I did not have titled, was probably somewhat under $10,000!

So at 10 a.m. one Friday morning, I was advised by Mr. Schweppe that I would have to find new employment at years end. By 10:15 a.m. that very morning, I was hired by the King County prosecutor's office, being recruited by my opponent in the "blue laws" cases. We happen to be meeting for coffee the same morning, and I told him of my imminent unemployment and availability. He took me directly over to his office, introduced me to his boss, King County Prosecutor Charles O. Carroll, and I was hired on the spot at three times the salary I had an hour before.

# Chapter 7

# CHOOSE THIS DAY
# WHOM YOU WILL SERVE

*Ezek 36:26-31*

*26 A new heart also will I give you, and a new spirit
will I put within you: and I will take away the
stony heart out of your flesh, and I will give you
an heart of flesh.*

*27 And I will put my spirit within you, and cause you
to walk in my statutes, and ye shall keep my judgments, and do them.*

*28 And ye shall dwell in the land that I gave to your
fathers; and ye shall be my people, and I will be
your God.*

*29 I will also save you from all your uncleannesses:
and I will call for the corn, and will increase it,
and lay no famine upon you.*

*30 And I will multiply the fruit of the tree, and the
increase of the field, that ye shall receive no more
reproach of famine among the heathen.*

*KJV*

W hen I came to Seattle in March the year before from Washington DC, I needed to pass the State Bar Exam in order to be licensed for practice. As I prepared to study, I was afforded the opportunity to pay for the examination either $75 for one test or $175 for three opportunities to take the exam. Generally, students from schools outside Washington State usually take the exam two or three times, simply because there are many laws peculiar to Washington State they do not learn about in their out-of-state schools. Without hesitation, I forked over the $175 as my law school experience in Washington, DC concentrated upon federal law with no attention to peculiarities of Washington State law. There were two areas in which I had great concern about the bar exam. The first was in ethics as the state exam would emphasize local cases, far removed from the federal arena. The second area of concern was that of security instruments as I had not taken any of those courses in school.

When the day came for the exam, I reported to Meany Hall at the University of Washington along with about 380 other applicants. The bar exam offered two choices: one you could write the answers in a booklet in one large room or you could be in the typing room in another hall. I chose the typing room as my handwriting is illegible. A grave error was made by those monitoring during the first session of the exam. In the typing room they passed out the exam on security instruments, whereas in the writing room they passed out the exam on estate taxes. Those monitoring the exams decided the only solution was to eliminate both sections of the tests, because there was no way to tell if any students had discussed their exam questions with people who were in the other room during the lunch break. That eliminated 1/6 of the bar exam, something to my knowledge that has never occurred before. During the second session or afternoon exam, the questions were on ethics. The situations obviously had been taken by the examiner from cases in the Virginia

Bar Review which I had read frequently having gone to law school in Washington, DC. As a result, I was familiar with most of the cases and hypotheses upon which the questions were based. To my astonishment, I passed the bar exam on my first endeavor! The Lord's hand was upon me.

While working at the Schweppe firm, I received a letter from the United States selective service advising that I was granted a draft deferment by my local selective service Board, because I was in law school. As a consequence, I was advised that I am must enlist in a military service within 60 days or be drafted into the United States Army. Some lawyers in the Schweppe firm were members of a National Guard unit comprised entirely of lawyers attached to the military Judge advocates General Corps. They had an opening in their unit and encouraged me to apply. I was inducted into the sixth jag unit, and directed to attend training weekends once a month at Fort Lawton, Seattle. Additionally, each Thursday evening our unit would train at the Army facility at fourth and Lander as a supplement to the weekend training program at Fort Lawton. This allowed me to continue my work at the Schweppe firm and to fulfill my military duty.

Serving the Armed Forces was not a problem for me. In fact, I was proud but surprised that in my poor physical condition they accepted me. My brother Henry had an outstanding career in the Navy and my brother Charles was very proud to serve in the Air Force, until his death. My brother Butch had joined the Navy, but served less than six months before being mustered out, presumably because of alcoholism and drug abuse.

However, when training turned to handling weapons, I began to have an emotional response that I could not explain. I did not want to handle a rifle, nor was I comfortable with the instructions on the use of the weapon for reasons I could not verbalize. It just made me nervous and upset each time our training turned that corner. Everything else was fine. I did not like being in the company of people who exhibited macho behavior constantly and used expletives to punctuate their speech and treated others in a demeaning faction just for the sport of it. I would turn my mind to "listen, respond, and do your job" whenever on duty. Then the day came when they ordered us to the target range to fire our M-14 rifles for the first time. It was a Saturday morning in early July 1965 when we were taken to the target range at Fort Lawton. We were instructed to pick up our rifles and fire them at the target. I picked mine up and then dropped it. My sergeant came over and stood beside me and ordered me to pick it up and fire it. I dropped it a second time. He then stated that I needed to pick it up and fire it at the target or I would be put in the stockade. I picked the rifle up and pulled the trigger and immediately suffered a blackout.

When I awoke, I was strapped to a bed in Madigan military hospital at Fort Lewis with an IV in my arm and a psychiatrist administering sodium pentothal (truth serum). I had no idea how I got there. The doctor was asking me what was the last thing I remembered. I recalled a 14-year-old boy, breaking through the window of a basement workshop and crawling in and turning on the light. I remember seeing a series of mirrors arranged in the ceiling. I remembered seeing a number of Webcore wire recorders running on a workbench and I remembered seeing a shotgun wired to a table saw aimed at a door. And I remembered seeing Jesus Christ, standing in front of the door, preventing it from being opened. The door was shattered into splinters, the shotgun was fully loaded and wired to the door knob, and the king of the universe was standing between the shotgun and young boys certain death. There was no doubt in my mind that He was standing in front of the door. Though I had no idea what Jesus looked like or who He was or is, I was absolutely and instantly aware not only as to His identity and Kingship, but that He loved me unconditionally and had from the beginning of time! I comprehend how "every knee shall bow and every tongue confess He is Lord" at the appointed hour.

At 25 years of age, I had suppressed all of those events from when I was 14 years of age into the dark recesses of my mind. I had not spoken with anyone, counseled with any or had been given any tools for dealing with the deep pain and abuse I had endured. But it mattered no more. The hurt was gone. I was freed. There was no doubt in my mind, whatsoever, that Jesus Christ had His hand on me all of those years. There was no question whatsoever, but that He had clearly taken charge of my life and engineered all of the events to bring me through to this day. I owed my very life to Him, and I gladly gave it.

Three weeks later I was discharged from the Army Reserve "for the good of the service" in that it was clear I would never be able to handle a weapon in combat. The only deep regret was that I was not permitted to return to my unit and say good bye or explain my situation. It did not matter to me as I did not consider my comrades as close friends as yet, but there was one sergeant who had taken me under his care and for whom I had great regard. Yet 27 years later I was giving my personal testimony to inmates at McNeil Island Prison when my former sergeant came forward and gave me a big hug right in the middle of my talk. He was a Volunteer Chaplain at the institution, and an Episcopal Clergy!

Before fully enacting the discharge, the Army Reserve sent me to the Harvard clinic for a psychiatric examination. I spent two hours talking with their psychiatrist, who then exclaimed that I had several issues he could address, including severe financial problems and he wanted to see me three days a week at a cost of $75 per session. I responded that I knew of one way to resolve the severe financial problems and that was to not come back! (So just who's crazy?...) I did not go back. I then received two notices from the Army dated the same day, one containing my discharge, and the other directing me to report to Point Roberts in California for basic training. I elected to believe the discharge and ignored the directive to report to California.

With a renewed fervor, I redirected my life, and now served my Lord and Savior Jesus Christ. I gathered as many books as I could find about Jesus, and I began to read everything I could, applying the study skills I had honed in seven years at college. I gave everything I had to the Lord. Tithing did not make sense as I knew that I did not owe just 10% of anything to him, as everything I had came from him. My approach was all belonged to him from which I tried to use less than 50%. Within six months, I had accumulated a wealth of information to permit me to truly worship, adore and serve my Risen Savior. Up until my episode at Fort Lawton, I knew very little about the Bible or the Lord. My episodes at church previously had been most unsatisfactory, having been thrown out of the Catholic Church and the Presbyterian Church respectively, as a child. I joined a Methodist Church in Walla Walla in college as a way to meet friends but found my awkwardness at social life plus their hypocrisy in lifestyle (for that church at that time) left me unfulfilled. I went to a Presbyterian Church for a while but had no grasp of true faith and belief in God. It was the moral life standard I was seeking and I found it no where in my experience. I knew the Christmas story in general, but I had no understanding of the relationship of David to Jesus, where that massive flood and Noah's Ark fit in, or what the significance of Easter was. Basically, I knew nothing. It was wonderful to now open my mind and fill it with knowledge of how the Lord has resolved our sin nature and defeated death. I began to attend every church meeting and every lecture and teachings series I could to give me the information I needed to understand and worship and serve God. Clearly, He had loved me from the very beginning of time, and He had His hand on me all of those years. I could not do enough to now show Him my love in return.

I joined the local Presbyterian Church, coincidentally the same one I had been thrown out of years before, and rose to the position of Deacon in short time. Through correspondence courses and seminary classes I brought myself up to speed as rapidly as I could. Church history was fascinating, as was eschatology. Life now had meaning and suffering had a purpose. As a boy, I had often dreamed that God was somewhere out there, amused by His universe and manipulating us like puppets for his entertainment. I had always known there was a god of some sort, but certainly not a personal savior or a loving caring creator that I now knew.

In a few short months, my awe turned from just recognizing my God to personal worship.

I dared to ask of my Lord two requests:

First, I asked that he would create in me a clean heart, remove the darkness that pervaded my life, permitting me to love others. I had been unable to love or be loved for as long as I could remember. My fear of people and what they would do if they found out about my background led me to avoid them at all costs. But I was lonely. I was friendless. I was wounded. I needed people in my life, and I needed to learn to trust them. I asked Jesus to give me the gift of love.

*John 13:34-36*

> *34 A new commandment I give unto you, That ye love one another; as I have loved you, that ye also love one another.*
> *35 By this shall all men know that ye are my disciples, if ye have love one to another.*
> *KJV*

He did, instantly! It was like the difference between night and day. The moment I asked, He took my heart in His hands and He caressed it, cared for it, loved it, bathed it in His blood, and re-created it clean and pure. Ever since that moment, I have had a love for everyone. I have never met a person I did not love instantly. I trust everyone immediately, and I want everyone to know Jesus. When the Kuwait War began and television images of tank battles reached our screens, I felt pain each time I saw a tank exploded, knowing some mothers child was inside, no matter whose side they fought for. When the twin towers went up in that horrendous attack, I could not help but weep for all the hatred being birthed by victims, attackers and sponsors everywhere. Wars are political, not moral. Each Soldier is as important as any other human being, no matter whose army or whose cause. Perhaps more valuable because of their courage in going into harms way for others. I fail to understand why children are permitted to play war with toy guns or violent video games killing perceived enemies. Competition is good and healthy. Maiming your fellow man is insanity. I understand that our sin nature has led us far from the Garden of Eden and that we need to defend and protect ourselves and our families from others as a practical matter, but this course is killing our souls with each new generation. I admire and honor those who fight for us and I cherish our liberty, but I weep that it is necessary to do harm to others in the course of life. Satan has captivated reason from our lives.

I have the same reservations with those who belittle their lives, demean their bodies or destroy their potential. Those addicted to sex, drugs, alcohol, pornography, power, violence, fame, greed, gluttony, or any other perversion are simply missing life! God gave us pleasure in procreation that we would enjoy creating children. He never intended our minds to focus so much on sexual conduct, create a sport out of the act, and use it outside the family, or exchange money or goods for its employment. Those who become obsessed to the exclusion of a healthy well-rounded existence are using perhaps 2 or 3 percent of their brain potential for lust to the exclusion of 97% of many other greater joys God has given us. Those who abuse food, alcohol or other drugs are exercising such a small percentage of their potential that the body dies within and the rest of the brain simply goes to sleep for lack of use. What a tragedy to waste your potential in such frivolous pursuits. The enemy wants to get his hooks into us as teens or younger because that is when the body develops its appetites. Our judgment is not yet mature and we usually are doubting our self worth and then along comes a drug or booze or some Madison-avenue heralded form of physical attention or worship and an endorphin is released in the brain. The unsuspecting victim says "whoopee" and seeks more and more of the same pleasure, not realizing he or she is ignoring literally thousands of other joys God has for us when we live up to our potential. And along come the media and some greedy folks ready to exploit the young. That millstone Jesus suggested be placed about the neck of anyone corrupting or detouring the vulnerable, the young, the lame, the disabled, the poor, the ignorant, the down-trodden, or whatever, should be put to use on their necks! We need to excite the young on their potential, open their minds to the possibilities of full life, and encourage and reward moral conduct. Too often we stand by as the media makes light of, or ridicules, the kids that grasp true under-standing and pursue moral virtues. But you know God gave me the ability to love them all. Prisoners, drunks, addicts, hoodlums or whomever. I have the capacity to love them and separate their souls from their sin. As a consequence, I have witnessed to murderers, rapists, terrorists and the tormented without passing judgment. It's a special gift. Speaking with a rebel who admitted he killed hundreds simply because of their race, a terrorist who tore open the chests of victims and ripped out their hearts, con men who embezzled millions from the poor...I can still find a path to their heart and share Jesus with them. Women who have had several abortions, parents who abandoned or abused their children and the children of others...The Lord wants their hearts, their repentance, their minds to be won back from the enemy.

My second request of my Savior was that I asked Jesus to restore my family. It seemed everyone had a family but me. I wanted my brothers, I wanted my mother, and I wanted my father! And I wanted them for eternity, as a family in Christ. That was my second prayer. This was not put as a test or challenge. I do not test God. It was not a bargaining tool. It was my hearts desire and I knew He loved me and would give me my hearts desire if it served His plan for my life. I would not question His response because God is God. But if you do not ask, how can you receive?

He did. He promised in His word that He would restore what the cankerworm has eaten away.

*Joel 2:25-29*

> *25 And I will restore to you the years that the locust hath eaten, the cankerworm, and the caterpiller, and the palmerworm, my great army which I sent among you.*
> *26 And ye shall eat in plenty, and be satisfied, and praise the name of the Lord your God, that hath dealt wondrously with you: and my people shall never be ashamed.*
> *27 And ye shall know that I am in the midst of Israel, and that I am the Lord your God, and none else: and my people shall never be ashamed.*
> *28 And it shall come to pass afterward, that I will pour out my spirit upon all flesh; and your sons and your daughters shall prophesy, your old men*

*shall dream dreams, your young men shall see
visions:*
*29 And also upon the servants and upon the hand-
maids in those days will I pour out my spirit.*
*KJV*

This took years, but I never doubted He would do it.

I started with the easiest one to find in my family, my
brother, Henry. He was now a lieutenant commander JG in
the United States Navy, stationed at Rota Spain. I wrote to
him and told him what Jesus had done in my life. I told him
that I forgave him for all of the things that he did in my
life and asked his forgiveness for those things and thoughts
which I had entertained. He wrote back and said that he
had accepted Jesus Christ as his Savior. Not only was he a
believer, he was dedicated to a strong discipling church and
attended Bible courses regularly. As commander, he helped
establish a chaplaincy on the Navy Base. His wife taught
Bible Studies to other Navy wives in their home!

My next brother, Charles, presented a bigger problem.
You recall he died in an automobile accident while stationed
at Lackland Air Force Base in Texas back in 1955. That was
just five days before he was coming home to help me. But
the Lord promised that He would restore my entire family to
me so I knew He had a plan. I prayed and asked for direction and the Lord brought to mind the box the Air Force had
sent back to me when my brother was buried. It contained
his personal effects. We had never opened the box. It was
simply placed in the attic. I went to the attic and pull it out.
Opening it, I found on top the American flag that covered his
casket at his burial. Directly underneath the flag was a small
pocket Bible. I opened it to the title page and there I found
his writing. Barely 2 weeks before his death, my brother
Charles wrote in his Bible that he accepted Jesus Christ as

his savior. It was finished. The Lord had indeed restored my brother Charles to me and we will be together in eternity.

My brother Butch was more difficult to locate. I had seen him on occasion through the years, but we did not have a strong personal relationship. From the time he went into Juvenile Detention, had become rebellious and estranged by his own choice from the family, and sort of wondered in and out of our lives. He fell into the trap of alcohol and drugs at an early age. He believed the lies of this world, that material things would bring happiness and hide the pain. He openly mocked my principled lifestyle and moral choices. He delighted in using expletives, and shocking behavior in my presence. At one point he struck me with his fist in the heart, and left me lying on the front lawn. Our early years of being companions had given way to a life of rebellion and running from authority. Leaving after a brief stint in the Navy, he enrolled at Western Washington College and then ran off with the money my mother and I provided for his education. One night the police called looking for him and we referred him to Western Washington College at Bellingham where we thought he lived. We had been sending money for his classes and rent. The police called back to say he had not been there in two years, having dropped out the first quarter. This was typical of him in those days and led to the family pretty much letting him go his own way. As an adult, he had been in and out of jail for various bad choices and had been married and divorced five times. The only time he came around was when he was in need of more money, but the contrast in our lives made him uncomfortable in my presence. His term of tenancy in the family home, while I was away at school, resulted in considerable damage to the house and untold expense to me in making repairs. On top of that, he had never paid any of the promised rent, and he had borrowed considerably more money, digging a deeper hole for himself.

Yet I loved my brother Butch very much. I wanted him to enjoy Jesus in this life and the next. Without him, my family would be incomplete. I was unwilling to abandon him to the enemy. Searching for several years, I finally located him living on the streets of Tacoma, a homeless alcoholic. I brought him home and offered him treatment in an alcohol treatment facility as well as a place to live. After a few days, he ran off. I located him a second time, now living on the streets of Puyallup and in rapidly deteriorating health. The alcohol and drug abuse had destroyed his body and his mind. He again rejected my efforts to help. He refused to accept Jesus in his life. Instead, he believed the lies of the enemy, that the world had conspired against him and that he was born a loser, damned and sentenced to an existence of begging and pain. He blamed everyone else for his problems and sought pity rather than reform. Satan had told him that he was unlovable, and he believed it! His esteem was gone. I was so angry with the enemy for what he had done in stealing away my brother that I made it a point to pray for him every day. He knew where I was and he knew that I loved him and that I was willing to help whenever he was ready. I never made accepting Jesus a condition of my help, I just wanted him back in my life, trusting the Lord would do the rest.

Years later, I was sitting in my law office, one Friday afternoon when I received a telephone call from a sheriff's deputy in Spokane County, nearly 300 miles east of Seattle. He reported that my brother Butch was on a ledge of the Davenport Hotel, threatening to throw himself to the street below. In trying to talk him off of the ledge, they found out about me and our relationship. They asked me to speak with him over the telephone. I told my brother that at long last it was time for him to stop trying to carry the burden himself and to give it over to Jesus. I said that it was the moment when he had to forgive all and asked Jesus into his life is his Savior and King. The pain could only be stopped by Our Lord. Then I led him in the sinner's prayer over the phone, pointing out that he had made a mess of his life and believed the lie of Satan too long. The enemy promised happiness lay in material things, fame and drugs and booze, but the true happiness only was available through the creator who sought him from the beginning of time. My brother came off of the ledge and into the hotel at 4:00 pm where the deputies held him until I could arrive to bring him back to Seattle. I enrolled my brother in a 60 day inpatient alcohol treatment program at Riverton Hospital and I went and sat with him in the classes every evening until he completed the program. Through many loving members of our church he was accepted and found self worth for the first time in his life. I provided funds for him to open up an office as an IRS appeals advocate. He worked with me in prison ministry, and in street ministry where we were privileged to bring many of his street companions and homeless friends into right relationship with Christ. It was a thrill to have him witness to inmates in the Monroe prison during Kairos prison ministry weekends. It was my joy to baptize him and lead him into a life worth living. Each day that we were not together, he telephoned me at 4 p.m. to tell me that he loved me and he loved Jesus. After four years, at age 52, he suffered a massive heart attack and went home to our Lord. Those four years that we had together were among the happiest of my life. In prison work his testimony spoke to many of the inmates, because of his street experience, drug and alcohol abuser, and broken marriages; he had insights none of the other team members had. Years later, inmates still ask me about him when I will return to the chaplaincy program.

My mother moved from Albuquerque to Las Vegas, Nevada. I wrote to her about the change that had come over my life now that I realized Jesus had His hand on me all those years.

Her life had changed as well in that her health had deteriorated to the point where she was on extensive medication. Her smoking and drinking had extracted such a heavy toll on her body that she now lived on a strict health regimen which included full abstinence from alcohol of any kind. When I went to visit her it was a delightful surprise to find her completely sober. I could not remember a time in my earlier life when I had truly known my mother as she really was... Her mind was now clear and receptive. We were able to joke and laugh and enjoy the love of Jesus for the first time I could remember. I could see the destruction and havoc the enemy had visited upon her life for many years and I could see the healing coming into her through our precious Lord. He was redeeming the years the cankerworm had stolen from her life as we spoke. The young girl who left home at age 19 to marry a dashing rodeo star, had left the sanctity and safety of her family and church, only later to fall into the clutches of a schizophrenic paranoid, was regaining life in an abstemious world. Those years of training at St. Paul's Episcopal school in Walla Walla had been regained. Free of the controlling nature of both poor-choice husbands, her spirit was coming out of the sleep induced by those two disastrous marriages. Now she was free again to find her Lord and the live the victorious life, appreciating the gift of four sons God gave her. From 1969 until her death in 1982, we had many good times together. Her sense of humor was a mirror of mine as we exchanged puns, jokes and quips all the time. She chose Las Vegas as her home town because of the many amusements and entertainment geared to senior tastes. She felt she was at a party when she visited local casinos and restaurants, but her "gaming" was controlled and she never lost much or won much. The impersonal relationship with a mechanical poker machine gave her hours of entertainment. That plus the warm weather, her puppies and modest home made retirement years comfortable. Because of the Las Vegas vacation travel packages, we could visit her often. Most nights I came we went to Jai Lai at the MGM Grand Hotel or the Silver Nugget neighborhood casino. Getting her into church was another matter. She did not want to socialize with others but she did read her bible, do daily devotions and read the bible lessons I sent. She was befriended by a Catholic Priest in the neighborhood who understood her personal choice not to attend church. He would stop in about every two weeks to visit, would play her piano and discuss my bible lessons with her. Indeed, The Lord had now restored my mother to me, and there was but one left to find to complete my family.

In 1958 I learned my father was released from Western State Hospital under an agreement that he report to a mental hospital in Los Angeles entrusted to his immediate family who were assuming his custody and care. He was to be institutionalized in California but was pronounced no longer a danger to others by the medical staff at Steilacoom hospital Washington. Being released on a pass in order to travel to California, my father asked to visit with me briefly in downtown Seattle. I met him at the bus station at eighth and Stuart and we had lunch at the counter while he explained he was being treated by the family physician in California. Our visit was cordial but superficial and when we were about to part he asked to take my photograph in a photomat machine. Thirty one years later, he still carried the photo in his wallet when I received his personal effects from the mortician. After he left me at the bus station I had no further contact with him until I went looking for him in 1967.

I wrote letters to the last address I had for his parents in California asking where I could find my father. They did not answer, but one day I received a telephone call from my dad, who was then living on Orcas Island in Washington State. We arranged to visit and my wife and two children journeyed the 80 miles north and took the ferry to Orcas Island. My father had not changed a great deal in physical appear-

ance from when I saw him at the bus depot, nor was he free
of the paranoia and schizophrenic behavior, but he appeared
contented and very pleased to see me again. I found out a
great deal on our first visit. He had hired people to report on
me ever since he had been released from the mental hospital
to go to California. He had never actually entered the mental
institution in Los Angeles or received any treatment after
leaving the state of Washington, contrary to the promise of
his parents and himself. They simply sponsored his expenses
in Los Angeles, having freed him from the mental hospital.

It was he who paid a college student in my dormitory
to report to him about me during my four years at Whitman
College. I was being spied upon through my college years
which explained the intrusions into my dormitory room and
apartment. He had subscribed to both the Seattle newspapers, in order to read of my trials while I was a King County
deputy prosecutor and he was aware of my marriage and the
birth of my daughter, but not of my son, who was adopted
(but only minutes after his birth) and therefore not reported
in the newspapers. He had the can of Copenhagen snuff left
in my room at college, because he felt it would bring to my
mind remembrances of him in better days and rekindle my
relationship with him. Clearly he still loved me but just as
clearly he was still very sick and delusional, making our visit
strained.

My endeavors to speak of Jesus fell on deaf ears with
my father and with his current wife. She had been married
four times previously and widowed four times, resulting
in considerable wealth for the two of them to live out their
fantasies and paranoia. Their lifestyle was to travel between
their home on Orcas Island, a cabin situated on Bell Island
which they also owned, located in the San Juan Islands, two
motels she inherited in California, a triplex they owned in
Las Vegas, and a horse ranch they were building in Williams,
Oregon. The ranch was started so that my father could experi-

ment with his inventions in solar energy and water treatment. Theirs was a comfortable lifestyle, but clearly their lives were haunted by perceived dangers and conspiracies. They were well suited to each other in their marriage relationship. Both suffered from acute paranoia and my father's schizophrenia was quite evident as well. They were under no medical care or psychological treatment for their mental conditions. They were simply consuming copious amounts of beer and wine. The Orcas Island home had one way glass windows in several guestrooms from which they could spy on visitors; there were collections of tape recorders and red-painted light bulbs evident in the workshop area as well. Sadly, his wife Nan took exception to our visit, being visibly uncomfortable sharing my father with anyone. Two hours into our calling upon them, she demanded that we leave the island and not return. Dad had invited us to spend a week with them and we arrived in our camper fully equipped for the stay. It was disappointing but clear that we had to leave in order to make his wife at ease once again. My father secretly established a second post office box at East Sound on Orcas Island so that he and I could continue to communicate without incurring her wrath.

We returned to Seattle, and I resigned myself to praying for my father as I had done for my brother Butch. I claimed the promise of Jesus that He would restore my entire family would be fulfilled and I never felt for an instant Jesus would fail me. The years went by, and in 1978 dad's wife passed away. I was now free to contact my father openly, but he again expressed no interest in learning of Jesus. He hired me to clear the estate of his late wife, and he took up residence with his housekeeper of many years.

It was in 1982 that I heard again from my father. I received a phone call from the housekeeper, advising that my father was in Los Angeles, California and asking for my help. He was critically ill with cancer and in great pain. He asked her to telephone me to come and help them. I took the plane to Los Angeles where they met me at the airport.

He asked three favors he wished of me:

First, he was dying of cancer, and only had a short time to live. As his only son, and only heir, he wanted my permission and blessing to marry his housekeeper, thereby disinheriting me. He acknowledge that he owed me a great deal and had never provided for me in any meaningful way all of my life. He was worth a considerable amount of money but he was very much in love with his housekeeper and wanted to provide for her, knowing that he was dying. Because of this dilemma he felt it important to have my consent to being disinherited.

Secondly, he wanted me to drive the two of them to Las Vegas, Nevada where they could get married without any waiting period. Because he was classified as mentally ill in California, he could not get a marriage license in that state, nor would he have time for the necessary blood tests required by law as he knew his time was short and he desired to complete their Union as soon as possible. He knew that if he were married to his housekeeper, she would enjoy considerable tax advantages both under federal and state laws and would be well provided for in her declining years. Nevada had no waiting period or required blood tests for marriage and he had no official recognition of his mental illness in that state.

Thirdly, he requested that I draw a will for him, securing the bequest of everything he had to his housekeeper. Without hesitation, I agreed to all of these requests, knowing it would give me one last opportunity to present Jesus to him. I did not need nor desire his accumulated wealth and I wanted to do all I could to make him happy in his last days. This life has been filled with torment and this would give a little pleasure to him in his last moments on earth. I believed that if I treated him in a Christian manner it would be one last opportunity to witness, in hopes that he would come to Jesus.

## Chapter Eight

# REDEMPTION AND COMPLETENESS

*1 John 5:2-9*

*2 By this we know that we love the children of God, when we love God, and keep his commandments.*

*3 For this is the love of God, that we keep his commandments: and his commandments are not grievous.*

*4 For whatsoever is born of God overcometh the world: and this is the victory that overcometh the world, even our faith.*

*5 Who is he that overcometh the world, but he that believeth that Jesus is the Son of God?*

*6 This is he that came by water and blood, even Jesus Christ; not by water only, but by water and blood. And it is the Spirit that beareth witness, because the Spirit is truth.*

*7 For there are three that bear record in heaven, the Father, the Word, and the Holy Ghost: and these three are one.*

*8 And there are three that bear witness in earth, the
   spirit, and the water, and the blood: and these three
   agree in one.*
*9 If we receive the witness of men, the witness of God
   is greater: for this is the witness of God which he
   hath testified of his Son.*
*KJV*

That my father had contracted cancer came as no surprise. For a former boxer, he was uncharacteristically inattentive to his health and physical being most of his life. Severely overweight, and having smoked and chewed tobacco for many years, and abusing alcohol, it was inevitable that his body would give out. Yet, he had lived well into his 80s'! It was sad to see the pain he was undergoing. There was no question but that I would do all I can to help him, because I loved him dearly despite his inability to parent me in an appropriate way. His mental impairment, which had lasted most of his life coupled with his abuse of intoxicants made it difficult, if not impossible, for him to comprehend his Creator. He evidenced a lack of trust the most everyone, seeing plots to take his wealth and tricks to deprive them of comfort in every corner. The government was his sworn enemy and the source of many perceived microphones and spy mechanisms in his small world. The reason he and his wife had so many homes was to keep traveling so that they could not be easily monitored by those they perceived as spying upon them. He had placed steel plates and foil about the parameters of their homes and vehicles to thwart eavesdropping he was certain was being attempted. Obviously he was not of sound mental capacity nor had he been all of my life as far as I could tell. Because of this I anticipated compassion in our Savior in dealing with my father but I also believed he must acknowledge Jesus in order to be saved. I saw this as my last opportunity to introduce him to my Lord.

Canceling appointments in my law office for the next few days, I had them execute new wills leaving everything he had to his intended bride in contemplation of marriage. At her request I set up the estate as a trust so that she would have a good financial advice and counsel in managing the inheritance. We then outfitted a vehicle with his oxygen and medical support equipment and headed across the desert towards Nevada. We reached Barstow, California, at midnight. Located in the high desert area, Barstow is famous for a large Black rock rising above the desert floor that can be viewed for miles around. Parking in the lot of an all-night restaurant, my father noticed a road sign at the base of the rock, which read "Jesus Christ, the same yesterday, today, and forever". The sign had been placed by "Chapel Of The Air", a radio program featuring John D. Jess, which I had been supporting for years. I listened every morning to Mr. Jess and enjoyed his teachings so much that I had been sending monthly donations to his radio show for several years. When my father mentioned the sign I seized the opportunity and proceeded to tell him all that Jesus meant to me in my life. I explain how the Lord had had his hand on me ever since I was a little boy. All of my early years he kept me safe through so much danger and neglect. With a heavy heart and an enduring love, I explain to my father that I had one last wish of him to fulfill my every dream: that was to bring him, my father, into right relationship with his Creator. Tears in his eyes, at age 85, my beloved father got on his knees in that Denny's parking lot and ask my forgiveness. More importantly, he asked Jesus into his heart, confessing him as his Savior! Hallelujah! The Lord had restored my entire family to me. I now know both of my parents and all of my siblings will be united again for eternity in heaven. Henry, Charles, Butch, and both of my parents had all acknowledged Jesus. From July 11th, 1965 when I first asked Jesus to bring me my family, it had been 23 years but he indeed had answered my prayer

We journeyed on into Las Vegas, Nevada, and I spent the evening with my mother while the rest stayed in a hotel. I explained to my mother the purpose of my trip, and while astounded that I would be with my father and his company, she graciously picked a bouquet of flowers from her Rose Garden for me to give to the bride at the ceremony the next morning. Clearly, the Lord had graciously removed all bitterness, between her and my father, in itself a miracle. They spoke briefly in the driveway when my father came to pick me up for the wedding and my mother wished him every good thing in his life.

Following the civil ceremony at the clerk's office in Las Vegas, I returned my father and his bride to Los Angeles, wishing them well. Three days later at Riverside Hospital my father went home to be with the Lord. At the request of his widow, I managed his estate and found a new home for her where she became part of our family. She did not want to stay in any of the houses or properties he had owned or acquired through his previous wife's estate, wanting a fresh start. I liquidated the properties and bought a home for her 2 miles from mine and she was incorporated into our family. To this day, she lives nearby, and we are in frequent touch. She knows our Lord and Savior, and we had the privilege of taking her to the holy land, China, Europe and throughout the Northwest as part of our family vacations. It was a wonderful blessing to have this lovely lady with us in our family and to show her so much of the world. She was from Oklahoma and had come to California many years ago for work. She found employment in doing laundry and as a motel maid for years and never had had the opportunity to travel or see the world before. It was a joy to see how the Lord provided her with the means through my father's estate to have a comfortable life. To this day, she remains grateful, and obedient to her Savior and Lord. I have never regretted my relinquishment of his wealth or properties, having traded the material things of this world for the eternal blessings of the next.

In 1965, I met a wonderful lady named Susan, to whom I was wed in 1966. The Lord provided me with a woman with a heart for God. She served for years as church secretary, coordinated preparations for the Billy Graham Crusade, completed nursing school and worked in the Ministry, blessing many. In her later years she was troubled by bipolar disorder. This changed her faith walk, starting with the death of her father from Alzheimer's. We have two wonderful children, a daughter and an adopted son who both bring me great joy every day. As a mother my wife did a wonderful and unbelievable job in raising our children and in keeping our household, all while serving in ministry, managing our bookstore, working at Crisis Pregnancy Center, and being church secretary. It was through her encouragement that I first entered Bible Study Fellowship and later became a teaching leader in Bible Study Outreach. We also participated in many Catholic and Episcopal Cursillo weekends and I enjoyed the privilege of working in outreach Cursillo weekends for Methodist and Presbyterian Emmaus walks in Fresno and Sacramento. For those of you who may not know, Cursillo and Emmaus are lay programs that came out of the Catholic Church experience in Majorca, Spain in the late 40s. It is a presentation of Christ and his love to 40 candidates over the period of four days, living with them and emphasizing faith, study and action in your Christian walk. A team of about 60 laypeople and three clergy set aside four days to live with men and women and to be role models of Christ in action. The movement is all over the world now and is replicated in many denominations besides the Catholic, Episcopal, Methodist, Presbyterian and Foursquare churches I have been privileged to work in.

In the mid-70s, our Cursillo experience grew into the introduction of prison ministry in Washington State called

Kairos, a similar program which grew out of Cursillo, but adapted for prisons. I have had the privilege of serving in approximately 50 such weekend programs and have introduced the same type of programs in Hawaii, Australia, Romania, and Africa.

My lovely wife became involved in ministering to AIDS patients at the Bailey-Boushay House, a specialty AIDS residence in Seattle. I followed her in becoming a volunteer driver for several years, which afforded me many opportunities to extend Christ's love to otherwise rejected people. Susan adapted her nursing skills to serving at Bailey-Boushay while I worked more as a messenger, driver and sounding board for the residents.

In our early marriage, Susan and I devoted much of our time to serving in the church but beyond its walls as well. We knew that Christ was the head of our family, and we strove to serve him in as many ways as we could. She hosted luncheons and weddings for the church, and later became an administrator of the Renton Crisis Pregnancy Center, an abortion rescue mission in our neighborhood. I served on several boards, including seven years with Friends of Youth Griffin Home for adolescent boys, and for 13 years on the board of Seattle Christian School. Teaching Sunday school, we both served as leaders of the youth program at Lake Burien Presbyterian Church for four years.

As a deputy prosecutor, my disdain for deadly weapons served me well in prosecution of felonies in the King County prosecutor's office. Though I loved serving in traffic court and travel to the smaller surrounding towns, my talents were judged best applied to trial of robbers, rapists, murderers and burglars. I tried many high profile cases with great success and worked on trials, appeals and appellate motions involving Ted Bundy, Wheat and Aiken, and Roy Hicks. In 1967, I was promoted to Chief Deputy of the Domestic Relations Division, at age 28, the youngest department head

in King County government at the time. But this was more
an example of the Lord's intervention than of my ambition,
aptitude, skills or planning. I had worked for two months
in the domestic relations department when I first entered
the prosecutor's office, the training ground where all new
criminal Department deputies began in King County. I made
many friends among the civil servants who were career
workers in that department. Years later, Eugene Hooper, who
had been head of the Domestic Relations Division for over
20 years, suddenly passed away. No one was appointed to fill
his vacancy, and so I went to my boss, Prosecutor Charles
O'Carroll, and offered to help in that department because of
the case backlog, thinking he would assign me there perhaps
one day a week. Instead, the following Monday, he named
me as the department head of Domestic Relations, much to
my surprise. Three years later, this served me well when I
entered private practice, because I had established a reputation in domestic relations matters, including divorce, juvenile court proceedings, guardianship, adoption and child
support. I enjoyed the criminal cases and did not intend to
leave that area when I offered to help the backlog in Domestic
Relations but it just worked out that way. The time I spent of
my years of practice in the criminal Department placed me
before most of the judges of the King County Superior Court
in some high profile cases. The first case I was assigned to
in the criminal Department was to assist the lead criminal
attorney in a major murder trial. The second day of proceedings, he became ill and I was thrown into the fire before the
most particular judge in the King County Superior Court.
There were three defense attorneys as well as much media
attention on the trial. I was too scared not to cross all the t's
and dot all of the i's, resulting in a first degree conviction in
my first major criminal case. I remember visiting with the
defendant's family after the verdict, consoling his mother
and giving them a copy of the book 'Prison to Praise". This

was their sixth son to be sentenced to prison and they were devastated. Other trials assigned to me included first and second degree murder trials, armed robberies, burglaries, rapes and all matter of criminal mischief.

In my daily walk The Lord continued to teach me valuable lessons in His gentle way. As department head, I was provided with a vehicle from the county. My wife and I decided I should give away my car to a deserving family, as we had her vehicle for family errands. We found a deserving young man and his wife who had two children and were in need of a car so we gifted it to them. The following week, he drove through an intersection and the car was destroyed in the accident, though fortunately no one was injured. At first, I was upset that my little car I had cared for so well was suddenly destroyed. It was the first new car I have ever owned. Then the Lord made me mindful of the fact that when you give to the Lord, you relinquish all claim. It was his car to do with as he saw fit and there were no strings attached to the gift. I had no claim on it and no right to be upset that it was destroyed in an accident. Ever since then, all of my gifts have been without attachment of strings or conditions. Though I may want a certain result or goal from my gift, I have no right to dictate to the Lord on how it will be used.

My entering private practice was another episode where the Lord clearly directed my path. During the election for King County Prosecutor in 1969, I was appointed as one of the campaign managers for my boss Charles O. Carroll, inasmuch as I was one of three department heads. Initially, Mr. Carroll had decided to retire from public office, having served since 1948, the longest officeholder in state history and the most influential Republican in Washington state office. On the last day of filing for candidates, the powers at the Seattle Post-Intelligencer and the Seattle Times met with Mr. Carroll in his office along with the three department heads. The newspapers each pleaded with Mr. Carroll to run for one more term, pledging their support for his reelection. He reluctantly conceded to their intervention and placed his plans for retirement on hold. Following his filing for office, they embarked upon a crusade against his reelection, alleging corruption and malfeasance in office and besmirching his reputation. It was then that I decided I did not want any part of political office. He was soundly defeated, though undoubtedly thousands of newspapers were sold. No charges were ever filed concerning the alleged corruption of Mr. Carroll so no platform was afforded him from which to defend his reputation. A brilliant man and a dedicated public service had been sacrificed by the news media needlessly.

It was clear that I would have no position in the incoming administration of his successor and I asked the Lord's direction for what he would have me do next in my life. My wife and I had two children, and I had a family to support. Within minutes of my prayer, I received a call from a member of the King County clerk's office. He advised that he had been watching my career for several years, as he had been engaged by a private attorney in Seattle to seek out a suitable partner to take over his firm. I was amazed, and astounded to find the Lord had already prepared a place for me. Ironically, the attorney turned out to be Melvin Swanson of West Seattle, the gentleman who had handled my mother's divorce from my father. This coincidence is what led my brothers to believe for years that my mother had somehow purchased my law practice for me from Mr. Swanson. The irony was that while Mr. Swanson had represented my mother 16 years before, he had no recollection of her or her case whatsoever Within hours of meeting with Mel, we reached full agreement for me to come into his practice as a full partner without any buying requirement of any kind. I was provided with a full working law office, complete with library, staff, equipment and clientele, located in the center of West Seattle just 20 minutes from my home! I was required to pay nothing for the privilege of joining the firm and our arrangement was simply a sharing of expenses. Because of his advanced age, it was the desire of Mr. Swanson to work into full retirement, which he did in six months. He had been practicing law since 1944. I continued to pay a portion of my earnings to him until his demise, and at that time his widow told me the firm was mine and I owed them nothing more. Mel was very pleased that I preserved the practice and assumed responsibility for his former clients during the remainder of his life. This clearly was a plan devised in heaven. I now was the sole owner of a thriving law practice situated in the heart of West Seattle with a built-in clientele and a sound reputation in the legal community. It was well beyond anything I could have imagined or hoped for at my young age and experience.

The practice afforded me time for ministry as well as community involvement. In 1963 when I returned to Seattle, I purposed to serve the community in exchange for the privileges I had in getting through school. With my awareness of Jesus and his involvement in my life, this turned to a dedication to bring His Love to others. Through seminary correspondence courses I began to accumulate teachings and methods of helping others to realize their potential in Christ. These Bible studies, teaching forums and civic activities necessarily involved me in growing and learning more as well. The first step was to start with Bible study programs and meaningful prayer groups. Apart from Bible Study Fellowship and Bible Study Outreach programs, I took the Bethel Bible Series through a good friend, Father Jon Lindenaeuer, an Episcopal priest at St. Elizabeth's Church in Burien. A two year course, The Bethel series gave me a sense of Bible history that I gained nowhere else. It included memorization of scriptures, study of themes that run through the course of the old and new Testaments, and learning the methods and markers for finding Biblical truths.

Through friends, I was introduced to a Bible study and prayer group that met on Friday mornings at 6 a.m. Started in 1962 in preparation for the Seattle world's fair, the group's main initial purpose was to bring men together from various denominations to pray in preparation for distributing pamphlets and literature at the Seattle world's fair. The Burien group decided to continue on meeting after the world's fair was over, and has met every Friday since 1962 to the present day, now 47 years! Men have come and gone, and many have gone on to be with the Lord. For the most part, the group has maintained a steady attendance averaging 12 to 15 men. It has met at various restaurants, some of which are no longer in existence. Satellite groups have started in surrounding cities, and at one time there were companion meetings every Friday morning in eight cities in the Pacific Northwest. This prayer group has become a sounding board for my life. It continually tests me and causes me to grow as these prayerful man searched through the Scriptures, sentence by sentence. Presently there are eight different denominations represented and each member comes from a different church. We took seven years to study the book of Hebrews and five years on Genesis. Each meeting begins with the passing out of cards which have prayer requests for individuals, most of whom do not even know they are being prayed for by a group of men. Any member can submit as many prayer requests as they wish by filling out a 3 x 5 card. Often, others will ask us to add them to the prayer cards, and even our waitresses through the years have submitted prayer requests. When I am not in Seattle, I know the group is praying for me whereever I may be. They are my closest brothers in Christ and form the core advisory board for most ongoing decisions in my life.

Based upon the model of the Friday morning group, I started similar meetings while I was in the prosecutor's office, attended by people from the clerk's office, our secretarial pool, the Seattle Police Department, and the prosecutor's office. We never took attendance, nor did we advertise the group. The Lord just kept leading people to us.

In 1970, when I moved to West Seattle for my law practice with Mel Swanson, I started two groups in the West Seattle Junction, one on Tuesday mornings and one Monday afternoons. At a local nursing home I chaired a group that met on Wednesday mornings. Thursday's I joined Father Lindenaeuer for services at St. Elizabeth's Episcopal Church, and on Saturday mornings we held a Bible study at Mr. Ed's restaurant in Burien. Thursday evenings I taught new believers in a construction work shack in downtown Seattle. Having immersed myself in seven Bible studies each week, I found myself growing in a love for Jesus at a satisfying rate. My friends in the Bible study classes became instrumental in putting me into more community involvement. With my wife busy at the Crisis Pregnancy Center and Bailey-Boushay house AIDS hospice, we had a full life.

The charismatic movement was very strong in Seattle in the late 60s and early 70s. The Men's Full Gospel Fellowship was very active, as were The Christian Businessman's Committee International, Woman's Aglow Fellowship, and various other Pentecostal programs with which we were involved. Each Thanksgiving the Seattle chapter of the Men's Full Gospel Fellowship hosted an annual celebration at the Olympic Hotel ballroom. We would look forward to each meeting with great anticipation.

In the early years of our marriage my wife and I decided to host a Tuesday evening fellowship in our home. People would come from around Burien bringing potluck foods to our large house around five in the evening. By eight or nine p.m., we would have 20 to 30 people. We alternated teaching and several brought their musical instruments as well as prayer concerns. Around 10 p.m., we would lay out blankets in a bedroom for the children to lay down as the meetings went on well into the night. Usually breaking up by 2 a.m., we saw the Lord work in many lives with healings, prophecies, visions, and group and individual manifestations of the Spirit. It was as if we were a small Pentecostal Church unto ourselves. The Tuesday evening church programs went on for four years. We then joined a new Pentecostal Foursquare Church called Life Flow Christian Center which held Wednesday evening services, as well as Sunday services. Our Tuesday evening programs gave way.

Early in our marriage, my wife and I decided to visit the holy lands before our children were of such age that it would be difficult to travel. We made arrangements to go on a holy land tour hosted by the president of Kings Garden ministries. Trusting the Lord would provide, we made reservations for the trip. As the day approached for the final payment, I had no idea where the funds would come from to pay for this extravagant adventure. On the day when the payment was due, I received checks from three different sources, all unexpected, providing exactly what was necessary to complete the arrangements. I knew we were intended to go and I sensed we were embarking upon a new adventure leading to more growth in the Lord.

We met with the others on the tour, and with our host, and his wife. They were very gracious people, and we took a liking to them immediately. I studied for about six months in advance of the tour, with emphasis on the places we would be visiting and the Biblical significance of each. Once the trip was under way, it was everything we dreamed of and more. When we arrived in Athens, the gentleman in charge of lecturing for the tour suffered a fall and was unable to continue. Our host became aware of my studies in advance of the trip and had me fill in in impromptu fashion as we continued the tour. By the time the three-week journey was complete, and we had been to Athens, Rome and Israel, I was asked to accompany the same tour in subsequent years.

We made an incredible 11 annual trips to the holy lands on behalf of Kings Garden. We were privileged to host/assist another trip with First Presbyterian Church of Seattle, and one for our own church, Life Flow Christian Center.

We also accompanied our host on trips to The Philippines and China in 1980 and individually visited Russia as part of an exchange program with the Goodwill games in 1982. I made it a point on each trip to contact the underground church and to do as much research as I could on evangelism in the global setting. Little did I know the Lord was preparing me for a bigger work in just a few years. It is clear His hand was upon me in so many ways.

Susan was raised Roman Catholic but at the time of our marriage left that church and joined Lake Burien Presbyterian Church, where I was an elder. We decided before marriage to blend our church lives, with the blessing of her family and my pastor. However, for reasons of his own, the priest elected at the last of three pre-marriage counseling sessions to insist that I consent to raising of the children in the Roman Catholic faith, even though the church had previously waived that commitment to her father and family. Susan was incensed at his request in what she viewed as a betrayal of trust. If asked, I would have agreed to raise the children as Roman Catholic at that early point in my Christian l walk, but I was not given the opportunity to even discuss it. Susan told the priest off and stomped out of the counseling session without a word to me. She was very angry and had me drive her directly home to her father. I was told by her father to not call or try to communicate with Susan until he gave permission. I had no idea what was going to happen. Then later in the week her father called and requested that we hold the wedding at the Presbyterian Church instead of the Roman Catholic church. In barely 2 weeks time, arrangements were made and the wedding proceeded on; Susan left the Catholic Church over the incident. Sadly, many people in her family refused to participate in the wedding including the flower girl and the ring bearer. The local Catholic church withheld the sacraments from Susan when she attempted to attend there after we were married, and she eventually withdrew and joined the Presbyterian Church. It is sad that denominations take this approach. I have been ecumenical in my belief that there are true believers of the faith in many denominations including the Catholic Church although I do not agree with some of its teachings but that we have no right to judge the heart of another believer. Only Jesus knows their heart and their relationship to Him. I have been privileged to participate in fellowship and services in many denominations, including Roman Catholic, and I feel sad for those who believe for some reason their own church is the exclusive and only right church. They are missing out on a great deal of fellowship, love and richness in their faith. When asked, I generally describe myself as an "Epi-Presbycostal", having spent time in the Episcopal and Presbyterian Church as well as the Foursquare Pentecostal church though my present membership is in the Full Gospel Foursquare Church International.

# Chapter 9

# The Books of Life

*Deut 30:5-10*

5 *And the Lord thy God will bring thee into the land which thy fathers possessed, and thou shalt possess it; and he will do thee good, and multiply thee above thy fathers.*

6 *And the Lord thy God will circumcise thine heart, and the heart of thy seed, to love the Lord thy God with all thine heart, and with all thy soul, that thou mayest live.*

7 *And the Lord thy God will put all these curses upon thine enemies, and on them that hate thee, which persecuted thee.*

8 *And thou shalt return and obey the voice of the Lord, and do all his commandments which I command thee this day.*

9 *And the Lord thy God will make thee plenteous in every work of thine hand, in the fruit of thy body, and in the fruit of thy cattle, and in the fruit of thy land, for good: for the Lord will again rejoice over thee for good, as he rejoiced over thy fathers:*

*KJV*

During the Vietnam War the Seattle area became a haven for many Vietnam refugees and for escapees known as "boat people" from Vietnam and Cambodia. One of the great needs in our area was for housing for refugees. A friend and I acquired a small house in Burien which we purposed to be used for the Lord's service. The mortgage payment was a nominal $200 per month. We leased it for the $200 payments to a Seattle drug rehabilitation program. Sadly, they abandoned the house after a year, and after failing to make most of the rent payments. When we went to reclaim it, we found it had been virtually destroyed throughout the interior. Working weekends and evenings, my friend and I put it back into good condition and then leased it to a family of boat people from Vietnam. The husband and wife and their children moved in. Within months, brothers and sisters of the father arrived in Seattle, and joined them in living in the small house. They divided the basement into apartments and built onto the back, of the house, creating family cubicles. They never missed a rent payment, and at the end of the final mortgage payment, we quit claim deeded the house to the family as a gift. They became a very productive part of our community. Ladies in our church tutored them in English as others worked in teaching homemaking skills. The wife became the accountant to a large restaurant chain. Two brothers opened an automobile repair shop in Ballard, which eventually grew to three shops. When the final payment was made and we transferred title to the house, they held a picnic for us on the back lawn, where we were fêted as guests of honor. Many Vietnamese from the community came to celebrate. We reminded them that the gift came from Jesus and not from us. We were very proud of the accomplishments they had made in our community in such a short time.

The experience with the Vietnamese house became a pilot project for four other rentals, I acquired in surrounding towns. It was a joy to see people growing in their faith and becoming valuable parts of the community. I purchased a duplex in Auburn and another in Kent which I rented at cost to help out people. Through the years several families that had been living on the streets as well as refugees and those recovering from addictions became beneficiaries of this program.

Before the days of the Internet, it was difficult to find the texts and treatises on Christianity I sought. Our small town had one small bookstore where I placed orders for several books that seemed curiously to never arrive. I confronted the owner one day, and he finally told me that he would not order the books, even though he had repeatedly said he had. He did not believe the books I ordered were consistent with his faith and his church teachings. They were Billy Graham publications and hardly controversial. I decided then that we needed another bookstore in our town. My wife and I began to pray about it and to set aside funds for such a venture. When we had accumulated $10,000 in our bookstore fund, the Lord brought a young man to my law office seeking help to incorporate a new Christian bookstore undertaking. A graduate of Oral Roberts University, he wanted to open a bookstore in Burien, and he had two other investors and needed one more investor for $10,000! Within hours, we had reached accord for incorporating and starting The Genesis Bookstore. As he searched for property to rent, I applied to the state to incorporate the name Genesis bookstore. Not surprisingly, the Washington Secretary of State responded that the name "Genesis Bookstore" was not available for incorporation, having been usurped by adult bookstores. With the consent of the other members of our enterprise, I reapplied using my preferred name of John 3: 16 Inc. "to be doing business as" the Genesis bookstore. I set forth the Lord Jesus Christ as the president of the corporation and the Secretary of State responded that that was not feasible as they required an address for all officers. I wrote back and told them that the

Lord Jesus Christ can be reached in care of his Father at any time! They acquiesced, and we were incorporated. Each of these four incorporating families designated a Christian beneficiary for the receipt of their share of the proceeds. In our family, we decided to supplement the income of teachers and faculty at Seattle Christian School, and to benefit the Crisis Pregnancy Center.

A lease was signed for the property in downtown Burien formerly occupied by the local newspaper. It was on the main street next to the Seattle Trust and Savings Bank. Next, we purchase timber at a lumber mill in the town of Gold Bar and built the shelving ourselves. Books and supplies were ordered, and within four months The Genesis Bookstore was open. It became an instant success. We expanded eventually to stores in Kent and Covington, at one time having 29 employees and managing in partnership 10 other smaller Christian bookstores. Because of this, we could buy our books in bulk and thereby become a supplier and lifeline in keeping smaller Christian bookstores in business that would otherwise not be able to survive. The Genesis became a center for prayer as well and source of provision for many in need. Susan was the assistant manager and served as manager of the bookstore for eight months when the manager was incapacitated by a skiing accident. She did a great job. We sponsored forums and lectures, brought in Christian entertainers to the Seattle Opera House such as Evie for an evening of music, and the artist and author Joni for a night of celebration of the Lord. We underwrote the performance of The Odd Couple at the Seattle repertory Theatre to benefit local food banks and a halfway house for teenage boys and we put on Friday night Christian Dance events including street dances, where we gave away Christian records to the young people. In 1990, I sold my interests in the Genesis bookstore to the employees in order to free myself for mission programs. The

Genesis bookstore has since sold out to a Northwest chain of Christian bookstores.

The Genesis bookstore became such a success, we decided to open a Christian lifestyle restaurant as well. We contacted an establishment in nearby Bellevue and a plan was undertaken to open 12 Baskets of Burien, Incorporating as "Five Loaves and Two Fish Company". We drew up a limited partnership agreement and plans that involved 12 equal investors. Once the 12 were assembled, we began praying and drawing plans. We located a site and preparations were underway with an investment of $8,000 each. The restaurant featured organic food and Kosher meats as a lifestyle example to people on good health as well as a strong faith. A small stage was built at one end of the restaurant from which student groups and Christian theater performance troupes presented entertainment. The Taproot Theatre Company of Seattle did the initial programs. The week of Christmas we had caroling, filling the establishment each evening. To serve the Lord, we set about hiring people who were recovering addicts and alcoholics as well as single mothers, and people in need of training in vocational skills. The restaurant was a great success for the first year, but then fell on hard times as the cost of organic food and Kosher meats soared. Since we had established the principle of healthful food from the very beginning, it was not feasible to now change, nor did we have any desire to conform to lower food standards in our meals. We elected instead to put the restaurant up for sale, and to close out our restaurant endeavor. The 12 baskets of Burien never did generate a profit in the worldly sense but that was not a major concern to me. Because some of the investors became unhappy with the lack of return, I offered to make them whole by buying out their shares for their original investment price. They accepted my offer and my total investment now was $68,000. Our business was bankrupt and we had no prospect for sale in the earthly sense or any foreseeable way to make up my loss. I trusted the Lord, and he provided another miracle. Nine months after the close of business, we were contacted by a man in Seattle, who owned a string of restaurants. He explained that his father insisted on meddling in his business of three successful downtown restaurants because he wanted to run a small restaurant himself. The man wanted to buy our establishment and reopen it under a totally different concept and gift it to his father. He offered me $68,000 plus reimbursement of the back rents! It was an incredible example of our Lord blessing me beyond my wildest dreams. In essence, a man came forward from nowhere and purchased the establishment for four times it's worth, without any question or concern. The Lord had made me economically whole and reinforced my faith that He was going to continue to do miracles in my life.

In my law practice I made it very clear to anyone that my faith in Jesus was paramount in my life. When one visited my office they found a Bible on the table in the waiting room along with other literature, and there was a portrait of Jesus on the wall and brochures concerning our Lord, nondenominational in nature, in plain view. I did not limit my practice to Christians, nor did I discriminate against those who were nonbelievers. I just was more comfortable serving those who were of the same mind as me so I tried to draw from that part of the community. I do not believe I ever pushed my beliefs upon anyone, but I certainly did not want anyone to think I was ashamed of the gospel at any time. Some clients responded by arguing with my point of view and others chose to go elsewhere for their legal services. However, there was no shortage of clients in my practice at any time. The one drawback was that many clients placed the little effort on paying their bill, expecting me to provide services without charge. However, the Lord always saw to it that there was sufficient income to meet our needs.

Few of my clients shared my deep religious beliefs but most respected them. On occasion, other clients would come to my door because of my outward expressions of belief. One such occasion was when a Lutheran pastor and our community brought me a letter he had received from a family back east. They were distraught, because a child they had received in shelter care had been abruptly removed by the authorities without explanation. It was a heartbreaking case and required as much prayer as legal expertise to resolve. The little boy had been found in a park in their city abandoned and covered with burn marks and other signs of abuse. "Jody" told them he was from Seattle, and he had been left in the park by his mother's boyfriend. He showed all the symptoms of a battered child. The authorities back east placed him with the family and their siblings, and they bonded with him over the months. He stopped the stuttering and became socialized and well adjusted within the family over the period of 18 months. Thee eastern state foster care authorities eventually contacted Washington State, and were advised the mother was in prison, and there was no apparent father figure, and therefore no interest by Washington State in bringing the boy back west. The family was advised that there was no reason why they could not seek to adopt the child. However, later, unannounced, a foster care worker from their home state appeared on the doorstep with representatives of Child protective services from Washington State and took the child from them, leaving them heartbroken. Their letters to the authorities in Washington remained unanswered for months, and they sought the help of the Lutheran pastor in finding an attorney to represent them.

I contacted the welfare department in Seattle, but was rebuffed and told there was no standing for this family to have any information about the child, and everything was protected by confidentiality laws. I brought suit in the King County Superior Court against the Child Protective Services, but the court ruled against me that there was no standing as my clients back east were not relatives to the child. I did not even know the child's true name or birth date. It was like a giant fishing expedition! They had poured their hearts out to the boy for 18 months under the promise that they could adopt him and now they were being barred from any information whatsoever.

One afternoon, one of the caseworkers in the Washington Child Protective Services invited me to their office Christmas party, presumably as a kindness rather than a sincere invitation. Something quickened within me and I accepted the invitation at once and went! While there, I asked several people concerning the fate of "Jody", and one of them told me they had been cautioned not to discuss the case of the boy with anyone. In their response, they inadvertently gave me the full name of the child and confidence that indeed he was within our district and being handled by the South Office of Seattle Child Protective Services.

Now having sufficient information, I brought a petition in the King County Juvenile Court for the state to show cause why the family whom had had the child for 18 months, should not have leave to intervene and apply for adoption. The clerk refused at first to file the petition, because it required assignment of a case number and the state authorities had to make those assignments from their records, not the court clerk. I inquired as to whether the number 0- 00-000– 00 had ever been used. The clerk said it had not and I applied that number to my documents and paid the filing fee. I then instructed the people back east to collect all their records and letters of reference and to provide photographs and any other information they had regarding their time with "Jody". I also told them to seek the prayers of as many faithful as they could to storm the gates of heaven that we might get "Jody" back. As documents came in, along with literally hundreds of letters of reference, I filed them with the Juvenile Court Clerk under cause 0- 00-000 – 00.

Several months later, I was heading to court at third and James to meet another client for an unrelated court hearing. As I was driving, something in my spirit alerted me that I needed to go in stead to the juvenile court at 12th and East Alder, some 4 miles east. I telephoned my client and postponed my hearing and proceeded to the Juvenile Court. Arriving there, I noted the docket, showing the case of "Jody" for disposition in courtroom III for leave to the state to place the boy up for adoption. I rushed into the courtroom and told the judge that I represented interest parties, and I had the clerk retrieve file 0- 00-000 – 00. The judge reviewed my papers in recess, and then postponed the hearing for two weeks to give me time to have my clients appear from the east. He directed the state to show cause why the child should not be released and returned to them as adoption prospects. The state's objection was simply that they had a bias in favor of Washington state residents adopting Washington State children. Buried in administrative rules and regulations, they could not see the bonding that had already taken place between the child and this very fine family who had already grown to love and nurture him.

Two weeks later, the entire family arrived from the east and stayed with my wife and myself. Their car literally died in the driveway of my house after having been driven across country. The following morning at the court hearing, the judge terminated the parental rights of the imprisoned mother, at her request and consent, declared the child eligible for adoption and placed him with my clients. A year later, the full adoption was completed.

There is no explanation, based in the law books or experience, other than the guiding of the Holy Spirit that can satisfy me as to how this child was reunited with his de facto family over a distance of 3000 miles without their even knowing his correct name, birthdate or residence!

On another occasion, I was appointed by the court to represent a young man named Dennis, who was charged with being the lookout and driver of a getaway car in a major bank robbery. One did not refuse appointments from the Presiding Judge to represent indigent defendants in criminal cases without jeopardizing their career. It was expected that all attorneys who served in the Prosecutors office would assist the court in taking defense appointments once they were in private practice. But when appointed, I learned my client was turning state's evidence against other parties in several other crucial cases. I went to the jail to meet Dennis and found him to be barely 18 years of age, extremely naïve, and obviously entangled in criminal activity as a consequence of being persuaded by his older brother, whom he idolized. He was frightened, and way out of his comfort zone in the criminal world. As had been my custom for years, I left him with a copy of Merlin Caruthers book "Prison to Praise", a very readable testimony of 96 pages about the gift of salvation from Christ and how to receive it. I have used this book for years with prisoners. He promised to read the book, and I promised to do what I could to have the charges reduced or dropped against him in exchange for his testimony for the state in other cases. The next evening I received a telephone call from his girlfriend. She told me she had been to see him in the jail and that he had read the book and had accepted Jesus. He gave her the book and told her to read it. She called to tell me that she had also accepted Jesus and that the book was being read by several other people within their family. She said Dennis was very grateful and trusted me that things would work out in his case and was willing to accept whatever the court ruled. Having no real viable defense to present on behalf of Dennis, I was baffled as to what to do for trial. I could not put him on the stand, but I did not want to see such a young man convicted of a major crime, where he had clearly been a pawn of others and had only acted as a lookout.

Arriving at the court for trial two weeks later, the case was called and the judge asked me where my client Dennis was. I told the judge that he was last seen by me in custody of the sheriff in the King County Jail. I had no idea where he was. The sheriff said they had no idea where he was either as he had been placed in witness protection and moved by the marshal's office to an undisclosed location. The judge gave the prosecutor, one day to produce the defendant. They could not, and the case was dismissed. I had kept my promise to Dennis and won my first criminal defense case since leaving the prosecutors office. Over the years I gave out so many copies of the book "Prison to Praise" that the author Merlin Caruthers started sending me cases of the book without charge from his nonprofit foundation.

# Chapter 10

# Gifts From Above

*Ex 6:2-9*

*2 And God spake unto Moses, and said unto him, I am the Lord:*

*3 And I appeared unto Abraham, unto Isaac, and unto Jacob, by the name of God Almighty, but by my name JEHOVAH was I not known to them.*

*4 And I have also established my covenant with them, to give them the land of Canaan, the land of their pilgrimage, wherein they were strangers.*

*5 And I have also heard the groaning of the children of Israel, whom the Egyptians keep in bondage; and I have remembered my covenant.*

*6 Wherefore say unto the children of Israel, I am the Lord, and I will bring you out from under the burdens of the Egyptians, and I will rid you out of their bondage, and I will redeem you with a stretched out arm, and with great judgments:*

*7 And I will take you to me for a people, and I will be to you a God: and ye shall know that I am the Lord your God, which bringeth you out from under the burdens of the Egyptians.*

8 *And I will bring you in unto the land, concerning the which I did swear to give it to Abraham, to Isaac, and to Jacob; and I will give it you for an heritage: I am the Lord.*
*KJV*

In the early 1970s my wife attended a prayer meeting with a friend of hers one Tuesday evening where there was a speaker from out of town. When she came home, she had clearly changed. The lovely shy proper Catholic girl I had married, was now effervescent, outgoing, and zealous, having received a Pentecostal outpouring. She spoke in tongues, experienced visions, bore the fire of prophetic word and was dramatically changed in an instant. I was envious. I believe the Lord gave her this special gift at this time and blessed her mightily as an encouragement she desperately needed to wash away the bitterness of her de facto excommunication from the Catholic Church and resulting estrangement from some family members and their friends. She did not bear ill will towards the Catholic Church but clearly she had been wounded by their rejection of her after a lifetime of attendance and schooling. One aunt in particular had gone out of her way to threaten Susan with banishment from all family matters and that she would burn in hell for eternity for having turned her back upon what she deemed "the one true church". This cruelty weighed heavily upon Susan and along with the refusal of the priests to serve her communion brought her into depression in the early months of our marriage. Now, the Lord had given her the special blessing of spiritual gifts, giving her the confidence of His continued acceptance of her and involvement in her life. The new tools helped her to accept herself and become a witness to others in her new faith direction. She started attending many charismatic events and exercised her gifts without hesitation.

Becoming involved in the Pentecostal movement, Susan made many new friends! I desperately wanted the same gifts for myself and sought them in every way I could. Friends prayed with me and tried to teach me how to receive this special indwelling, but for the present it was not to be. I attended the full Gospel Fellowship meetings, and every Pentecostal gathering I could, but it was not happening in my life at that time. Finally, I decided the Lord had given her this special anointing, because she needed it! Still, I did not give up hope, and kept praying for the indwelling of the Holy Spirit and charismatic gifts within my life.

The work I had done for years in warehousing and construction, and presumably the work in my own yard, when I built the rockery and tore down the remains of the burnt garage, had taken a toll on my back. I was beginning to suffer severe back pain. This was diagnosed as an arthritic degenerative bone condition by the doctors and deemed untreatable. They fitted me with a harness and provided pain medication but determine the portion of my back affected was inoperable. I was walking with my back arched over and could not stand straight after being seated for a period of time. Sleeping was very difficult as I could not find a comfortable position even though I employed several pillows and a back brace. Other than pain medicines, there was little they could do to relieve the pain. In 1975 the condition became intolerable and I began to explore alternatives to traditional medical treatment. Acupuncture and massage were of no help. Naturopathic remedies were not the solution. My friends and I turned to prayer. One evening I received word that the Lord was going to heal me in November. I focused my attention on the Thanksgiving Full Gospel Annual meeting in November as the likely time. I concentrated my prayer life on that date as the doctors had given up all other forms of treatment. The pain medications they provided permitted me to fall asleep, but if I was disturbed any time during the night, I could not have any further medication, and the pain would prevent me from going back to sleep. I could barely interact with my children. Court hearings were difficult, and even the drive to and from work was something I dreaded. As November approached, I became excited about the prospect of my being healed. Little did I know what the Lord had in store for me.

The week before Thanksgiving, we received word the Full Gospel meeting for the following Saturday before Thanksgiving was canceled! My hopes were crushed. I had focused on that meeting for months, knowing in my heart the Lord would be there and would touch my pain. Now, the meeting would not take place, and I saw "no hope" of being healed. But the Lord was teaching me and opening my eyes to even greater truths. He does not reside at meetings, nor does he require a gathering of others to perform his miracles.

Friday evening I went to bed after having taken my pain medication. At approximately 2 a.m. on Saturday, there was a car accident outside our house, resulting in fire trucks and sirens arousing me from my sleep. Disgusted, I got out of bed in my crouching posture and struggled to the dining room so as not to wake my wife. At the dining room table, I perched on the edge of a chair, leaning forward so as not to hurt my back, and opened my Bible. It found its way to Isaiah. I attempted to read the chapter, but the words were blurred. I cried out to God! Suddenly tears poured down my face. I felt like I was no longer in my body and I had no sense of feeling at all of anything. I asked God why? I asked why I had to endure the pain. I asked why I could not read the words of His book. I asked why the meeting had been canceled. Suddenly I could see the words in the Bible clearly. They were literally floating above the page. It was as if the type was separate from the paper. They were in bold print and sharp precise lettering. The words literally were strung together in a dance above the Bible as if drawn in a cartoon. I started reading them aloud. I began to feel my body lifting. It was surreal. I then felt myself suspended in air as though I was on the ceiling looking down at my physical body. I could see a flame going through my body starting above my head and going all the way down to my toes and I could feel the warmth and healing as it went. A white light shone out my fingers and went about my body as I watched it! And then a voice said speak, and I began to talk, but the words were not mine; they were unintelligible. I was speaking in tongues for the first time. I knew I was praising God, but I could not understand the words I was using. My spirit floated back like a feather into my physical being in the chair. I was sitting upright and there was no pain. I got up from the chair and started to walk around the table, back and forth. There was no pain. I turned the chair on its side and jumped over it, and there was no pain. I ran into the bedroom, babbling all the way. My wife woke up and at first thought I had suffered a stroke and reached for the phone to call the doctor. Then she realized I was speaking in tongues. My eyes were perfect and I did not need my glasses. I could bend and move in all directions as though I were a kid again.

After church in the morning we drove to LaConner to tell her folks and show them the change in my back and body. I had to tell people what was going on. We drove around visiting other friends and drove over and told my pastor. He gave me the privilege of testifying in the Presbyterian Church the next Sunday morning. Graciously, he permitted me to witness of the physical healing and gifts of the Spirit that I had received. I will eternally be grateful to pastor Richard Redfield for that Sunday morning. After the service he told me how happy he was for the gifts God had bestowed upon me but he suggested that I probably would never be satisfied in the Presbyterian Church with my Pentecostal anointing and that I probably should look for a new church home. He was a very wise man, and good friend. For me to have stayed in that setting would have been disruptive, stifling and a distraction and it was clearly time for me to move on to a new Full Gospel Church.

My wife and I tried several churches, and even expanded our own Tuesday evening services in our home. It was not until 1981, that we started attending a new church called Life Flow Christian Center, a small foursquare Church that had just opened its doors months earlier. I remain there to this day, the church has since undergone a name change to Westside Foursquare Church.

Several years later, on Super Bowl Sunday, I headed out the door for church early in the morning. Suddenly, I slipped on the ice and fell down the steps, landing a top the rockery on my back. Being unable to get back up the stairs to the house, instead I made my way to the car and drove on to church to teach my Sunday school class. My wife arrived an hour later, and seeing my injuries immediately drove me to the hospital. I had suffered three crushed discs, L 4-5-6 in my back. The pain was excruciating. Surgery became necessary, and the disks were fused. The question is often raised by others as to why the Lord chooses to heal some and not others and why He does on some occasions and not other occasions. I have been blessed to have been healed by the Lord many times, probably more than I realize. I know He healed me of gout and of Bell's palsy and of my back pain in 1975. On other occasions, He has not healed me of other conditions even though I have asked. Since He is God I have no standing to question His withholding or granting of anything. That He has already given His only son's life on the cross is more than I could have ever dreamed possible. What suffering I have endured in this life is nothing compared to what He has done for me. So as He blesses me with healings or with-holds in His wisdom, my response is to praise His name. Sometimes, I know He permits me to suffer, because I need the rest that my affliction dictates. Other times, I understand my testimony is all the more meaningful to others, because I endure a pain in my life without complaint and it becomes a witness to others.

1992 was a big year for health changes in my life. My daughter was serving as a missionary with Youth with a Mission in New Zealand for two years. As a wedding anniversary gift to ourselves, and a long needed vacation for Susan whose father had succumbed to Alzheimer's after seven years, we decided to fly to New Zealand for a visit at the mission where Maria worked and then to cruise across the Pacific to Tahiti and from there to fly home to Seattle. New Zealand was a wonderful experience. Boarding the Royal Cruise Line vessel, we then headed out for two weeks at sea, visiting several ports along the way. My wife loved to take cruises for vacation, and each year I tried to accommodate her with a sailing excursion. After we left Fiji, we dressed for dinner and headed to the dining room. The first course served to me was a mixed seafood cocktail. I loved seafood. It had been a favorite of mine for years. I enjoyed oysters, clams, shrimp, lobster, salmon, etc. This was a blend of seafoods in a sauce served in a small appetizer dish. I took one small bite and immediately noticed many purple bumps rising on the tops of my fingers on both hands. Recognizing that it must be an allergic reaction of some form, I immediately got up from the table and walked perhaps 10 feet to the staircase and down the stairs to the infirmary below. There I collapsed, unable to breathe. My body was already striped by several broad red rashes and there were assorted colored bumps throughout my body. The ship's doctor immediately started IVs and oxygen and kept me under constant surveillance while talking to the shore via radio for further medical advice. I was returned to my bed in the room and my body began to balloon up in size, much like a grotesque Pillsbury doughboy caricature. The bumps on the top of my hands were purple but those on the palms underneath were bright red, and itched unceasingly. To alleviate the itching, I rubbed a large cloth between the palms. This caused the hands to get red hot, and I then plunged them in a bucket of ice water. They would get freezing cold, and I would pull them out and the itching would begin anew. Whenever I turned in the bed. my skin stuck to the sheet and pulled away, leaving raw flesh. It was a nightmare! The ship's doctor visited nearly hourly and continued to administer medications and provide fresh linens and pillows. This horrendous condition continued and my body deteriorated by the hour. On the fourth day at sea, a wide black line started progressing up my spine. Reaching just below the neck, the doctor determined it was critical and asked people on shore to airlift me from the cruise ship to a land hospital.

With the assistance of the Coast Guard from Tahiti, I was airlifted off the cruise ship, wrapped in a sheet, carrying only my documents and Bible. The ships Purser, First Officer, and Dr. all promised they would visit me personally as soon as the cruise ship reached port at Tahiti and that everything would be taken care of. I never saw any of them again. No one from the ship made any visit or contact me in any way once I was removed from the vessel. They cleverly arranged for a skeet shooting exhibition on one side of the ship as they removed me on the other side so as not to alarm passengers. I felt like a leper being sent away in disgrace for some unexplained reason. Staying with our belongings aboard the ship, my wife visited me when the ship arrived four days later in Tahiti. But she had not been advised of anything by the crew, either.

From Mariana Island I was flown to Tahiti, and then taken by ambulance to the Pacifica Medical Hospital and placed under the care of a French doctor. The doctor knew a little English, but no one else in the facility spoke English. He explained that I was suffering severe allergic reaction and it was treatable in his opinion. When I was released from the hospital, the rash had disappeared, my flesh no longer tore off, and the bumps and itching had stopped. I still resembled the Pillsbury doughboy and had been pumped through with many fluids. The medical facility was satisfactory under the circumstances. My bed was a small and was equipped with an IV pole with one broken wheel. When they did the ultrasound the equipment was mounted on a large piece of plywood and had been constructed by the doctor from various pieces of equipment that resembled a high school science project. (I was amazed when I returned to Seattle to have the physicians there remark how good the ultrasound pictures were. I had little faith in them myself, having to hold the plywood and keep two parts from rolling off as the sounding was made). I was not interested in food and it was a good thing because for lunch they brought in a shrimp salad and for dinner it was salmon, neither of which I could touch because of the seafood poisoning. People talked to me incessantly in French which I did not understand and one lady insisted on changing my IV to the back of my knee because in the arms they could no longer reach the veins. This was a very painful process that was done by brute force because they could not communicate with me. Slowly the rash began to fade and the bumps went down as well as my fever over the next few days. I had sores over most of my body and I was filled with fluids to the point where it was difficult to even stand let alone walk. United Airlines took great care in returning me to California, and then Seattle, where I remained in treatment for the next six months. My medical expenses were at long last paid by the Royal Cruise Line and they invited us to be their guests on a cruise anywhere they went each year that we desired to go. I was no longer interested in going on the cruises. As a consequence of the seafood poisoning, I contracted diabetes and became dependent upon medications which I must continue to take to this day. I must avoid all seafood products and extracts and I carry an epi- pen with me at all times. The issue of being tested to find out which seafood was the culprit has been visited many times. However, my doctors advised me that once the nervous system is overcome by a particular poison it will not fight that same poison a second time should it be introduced into the system. For that reason, they will not test me for the precise seafood and I must avoid all such products.

I posed the question to my Pastor Harvey Oxner as to why the Lord revealed to Peter by the vision of the sheet that all things were clean to eat when clearly I cannot eat seafood. Harvey answered that I was not Peter. I do miss seafood, and it is an extreme inconvenience to try to avoid seafood and sea products when I travel. It becomes a big inconvenience to my hosts, particularly in third world countries where there are not a lot of choices for food. In the Philippines, and Africa in particular, it is very difficult to maintain a seafood free diet, but it is a cross I must bare. I have had four occasions where I have inadvertently received sea products, and had to result to employment of the epi pen, doses of Benadryl, and some visits to the ER.

While the Lord has showered me with good gifts from above, and provided me with healings and blessings I do not deserve, he has made me curiously vulnerable and suscep- tible to many dangers in my travels uncommon to others. The diabetes and the seafood allergies are difficult to defend against on a daily basis in other cultures. Yet, I live to serve Christ. As I have told my loved ones, for me to not travel is far worse than death. I feel blessed and have no regrets and continuing my missionary walk. The one event that sticks out in my mind was the decision of my wife to leave me in 1996. After 32 years of marriage and raising a wonderful family, she sought a life change. We remain friends to this day for which I am most grateful. I have never loved another and know I never will.

# Chapter 11

# My "Call To Macedonia"

*Matt 28:18*

*18 And Jesus came and spake unto them, saying, All
power is given unto me in heaven and in earth.*
*19 Go ye therefore, and teach all nations, baptizing
them in the name of the Father, and of the Son,
and of the Holy Ghost:*
*20 Teaching them to observe all things whatsoever
I have commanded you: and, lo, I am with you
alway, even unto the end of the world. Amen.*
*KJV*

In the early 80s our young family was firmly grounded in
the Foursquare Church at Life Flow Christian Center and
actively engaged in the Puget Sound Pentecostal movement.
We attended Christian bookseller conventions, full gospel
meetings, and various Christian out reaches. Our appetite
for Jesus and the works of the Holy Spirit were insatiable.
Susan worked as a church secretary to pastor Lawrence and
I preached as a lay minister at various missions in Seattle
and Tacoma. In the mid-80s our pastor asked several of us
to work on building the men's Fellowship in the church.

We undertook several activities including involving men from the church in our prison ministry programs, missions preaching events and doing charitable works for others in the community. Coupled with a strong reading program and prayer meetings, the Men's Fellowship grew. In July of 1987, on a Saturday afternoon, the men's Fellowship as a group attended a Full Gospel Meeting at a downtown hotel where a guest speaker from the Midwest was telling of his experience when he had escaped from a prison in Moscow, Russia. He spoke of how he managed to get away from the prison facility, and his efforts to escape the Soviet bloc countries back to the west. As he recounted his getaway, my attention was piqued. When his travelogue reached Romania, he said in a brief sentence something that astounded me. He recounted that in Suceavea, Romania, the Pentecostal Christians hid him in their home for four nights at risk of death to their entire family. I was stunned. I sent up an arrow prayer to the Lord. I said "if you will send me to Romania, I will be your hands and your feet". I told that prayer, to no one. I did not share it with my wife, with my pastor, or even with my best friend. No one in the world knew of my promise to the Lord except Jesus and myself. I knew literally nothing of Romania other than having a vague understanding that it was a cold war puppet state of the Soviet Bloc and a dictatorship. There are no Romanian connections in my family, friends or associates. But from what the speaker said, I understood there were men and women of God in Romania who were willing to sacrifice everything they had to help a stranger. It was enough for me.

2 1/2 years later, the Lord answered my prayer. The first hint of my being called to respond to my promise to God occurred on Christmas day. As I was walking to the kitchen in my house, I heard over the radio that dictator Nicolas Ceausescu had been assassinated in Romania. My heart quickened, and I instantly recalled my arrow prayer.

I had shared my promise, with no one and had forgotten it myself by that time. Involved in practicing law and providing for my family, preaching in missions and working in the church, entering the mission field was far from my plans. I was curious about the events in Romania and the rest of the Eastern Bloc, but I knew the Lord would *never* provide a way for me to go there! Then in March, I was working at my desk in my law office when I received a telephone call from my former pastor, now living in Colorado Springs, about 1500 miles away. I had not seen him in several years since he changed churches and moved to Colorado. He stated that he had received an invitation to go to Romania with a Romanian pastor then living in Frankfurt Germany. He wanted to go, but he had never been out of the United States, and he wanted me to accompany him for the journey because I was use to foreign travel. I immediately agreed.

Three days later, I flew to Colorado Springs. From there we flew to Frankfurt Germany, where I met Pastor Vladimir Caravan. Vladimir was a Romanian who had escaped from the Ceausescu dictatorship years before and had been living in Frankfurt, Germany, where he pastored a small church and engaged in smuggling goods, Bibles and medicines back into Romania and other Eastern Bloc countries. Now that the revolution was underway in Romania with dictator Nicolas Ceausescu assassinated, he wanted to show the conditions of his home land to American pastors in hopes of getting more help for his beloved native country. Pastor Lawrence and I were the first to be invited to accompany him.

We loaded his old yellow Mercedes station wagon and it's appended blue trailer with foods, clothing and medicines for the journey. With $1200 that I collected from my church, we purchased 600 Romanian Bibles to take with us. From Frankfurt, we drove to Nuremberg, where we picked up another passenger, brother George, who had frequently accompanied Vladimir into Romania over the years. Driving across Austria and Hungary, we reached the Romanian border at about 4 a.m. two days later. We slept in the car as the driving was shared, and we ate bread and cheese and luncheon meat for meals along the way. In eastern Hungary we visited a Romanian pastor who had a refugee camp where he cared for many who had escaped Romania over the years. His work was to hide the escapees and direct them to safe havens for the routes west. A beautiful man and a very brave pastor, it was an honor to preach in his small village church as our first introduction to Romanian worship. I can still see the glow on his face as we gave him a Romanian language Bible. The tears flowed as he opened the book, and read in his native language the words of our precious Savior Jesus. Most pastors we met in Romania had German or English Bibles or Russian Bibles: very few had Bibles printed in Romanian! We spent a day at the Hungarian house as Vladimir studied information on where we could safely travel in Romania, the road and police conditions and where we could be housed on our journey. Lawrence and I worked with some refugees, organized supplies in the trailer and prepared gift packets of food and clothing to give to families.

The Romanian border was a formidable sight. For as far as one can see, there were old vehicles in grave condition, trucks of supplies, horse drawn carts, gypsy wagons, bicycles, motorbikes and motorbikes with sidecars, people packing household goods and family treasures, herds of animals and livestock, ducks, chickens, goats, and endless lines of people of all ages all patiently waiting at the border on both sides. Clearly there were loved ones trying to reach family within Romania and relief agencies sending whatever they could to help the war-torn country. Coming out at the border were the young and the able bodied workers, many elderly, and many families. There was a sense of desperation to leave the country while they could and an opportunity to be grasped by the young for a promise of a better life in the West.

Within the country, once we had cleared the border six hours later, we found almost everything was in need of repair or replacement. Traffic signals did not work. Roads were nearly impassable or nonexistent. Stores had no supplies and petro was very difficult to find. Our vehicle was diesel powered so that we could use farm fuel when necessary. We carried two 10 gallon drums of diesel with us. The electricity did not work nearly everywhere we went and most homes were without heat unless they had a small ceramic fireplace in which to burn rubble, cardboard or corncobs. The water was putrid if the faucet worked. What few shops were open, had long lines of people waiting in hopes of getting bread at one queue and coffee at another. Clearly the old expression "It is better to be Romanian than patient" took on a heightened meaning for me. Yet the people were sensing a change and a new Hope, because of the revolution. The Latvian states, Poland, Hungary, and Yugoslavia gained their independence without bloodshed. For Romania, it was a different story. To this day, there is not an accurate count of how many thousands lost their lives in fighting for Romanian freedom. We do know the battle began in the western town of Timisoara when a courageous pastor called for public daily prayers at noon in the town square. The igniting event for the Romanian unrest was ousting from his home of a popular Hungarian clergy who had been openly critical of the Romanian authorities. This escalated into civil unrest followed by more official oppression. The Pastor from Timisoara commenced public noon prayers to encourage peaceful changes. With falling of Eastern Countries occurring throughout the rest of the Soviet bloc, there was no turning back. The Timisoara prayer vigils were held for several days from the balcony of the Opera House in the town center. As the crowds grew each day, Nikolai Ceausescu would not tolerate such insubordination within his country and ordered army troops and tanks to hide behind the Opera House and then come out and surprise the crowd in their prayer and demonstrations. When the tanks entered the square, they fired projectiles over the crowd, reportedly to "scare off" the people. Sadly, the shells struck young children at the end of the square as they were going into the Orthodox Church building. Many were killed and revolution was underway as word spread like wildfire across the country.

In Bucharest, the university students and others took up the battle cry. In an act of treachery, beyond comprehension, Ceausescu ordered his troops to emerge from the storm drains and fire machine guns at the crowd, killing hundreds and igniting bloodshed across the land. As the crowds gathered momentum, the military turned on the dictator and he was assassinated. A part of the Politburo, which ruled Romania from 1944 on, Ceausescu solidified his power by catering to the whims of Moscow in his early career. He rose to solidify power around himself slowly by 1954 and became the totalitarian head of the country in 1965, when he modeled his career and communist ideals after Chairman Mao. His dream for Romania was to create a state controlled labor force for manufacturing as a commodity to sell to the rest of the communist bloc. In order to do this, he systematically destroyed all competing enterprises, including agriculture, except for state communal farms. When the Chernobyl catastrophe occurred, Ceausescu ordered his people into the streets to parade in proof that there was no danger of radiation and that the world news reports were a fabrication of the Western media. When the radiation clouds hung over Romania, and people began to get sick and lose their hair, he told the people keeping a bowl of warm water by the bed at night would ward off any ill effects. Sadly, 15 years later, in some homes, you still find the lady of the house providing the warm water! The cruelty and atrocities of Nicholas Ceausescu are simply too many to detail here. He ranks right up there with Stalin and Hitler as personification of evil.

It was into this atmosphere that I entered Romania in March 1990. The first major city visited was Cluj. Situated in north-central Romania, Cluj is a pivotal city. A young family let us stay in their small apartment that evening, after we visited the large Pentecostal Church.. We preached of Jesus Christ crucified and of our love for brothers and sisters in Christ everywhere, bringing a message of hope to these people. For a late dinner we had Chorba soup and bread. The apartment was small even for the family so we slept on bed rolls on the floor, grateful to be indoors. From Cluj, we set forth the next morning after a breakfast of lard, black olives, green peppers and bread. The drive to Suceavea took us across the Humor mountains on to the north-eastern plains of Romania. We were welcomed by the administrator of the Pentecostal union churches in the Suceavea district, a man who had worked for years with Vladimir. He lived in a very old farmhouse situated within the town, and with a large adjoining warehouse in which were stored clothing and supplies. There were two small rooms attached to the house, which became our home for the next two weeks. I was given the one small bedroom with a single bed and a wooden chair as its only furniture. There was no heat, but that was common place for all. Pastor Lawrence, and George slept in the outer room and Vladimir was invited into the main house with the family.

On the following morning we were joined by a Romanian Pastor Ianos Nikolai. This gentleman used to be a world-ranked professional boxer and contender for the crown. He was barred from fighting internationally by Ceausescu because he refused to acknowledge the Communist Party. He became an outspoken critic of the regime and engaged in public evangelism and preaching in villages and large towns. On one occasion, he secured the Bucharest soccer arena and staged a four-day evangelism program drawing many to Christ. Authorities attempted to arrest him on many occasions; they would come into churches as he was preaching and look for him and he would be standing in plain view, and they would not see him. On other occasions they would stop a vehicle he was in and look but could not see him! He had been arrested several times as well but charges were always dismissed or evidence lost. He became a symbol of religious freedom for the multitudes and openly confronted the authorities for years. As we prayed together on the floor of that small room in Suceavea, he revealed many prophecies involving ourselves, our families and our future. It was an awesome time. He became one of my closest friends, and I count it a privilege to serve with him.

I quickly bonded with the Romanian Pentecostal people. Each home that we entered, the entire family would get on their knees and pray, thanking the Lord for our safe journey and asking his blessings upon each who was there. This opening welcome generally took 15 to 20 minutes at each home, and everyone participated in it, each of the ladies covering their heads with a scarf as they prayed. From the elderly and infirm to the little children and the farm hands, all got on their knees to pray when we arrived and as we left! Each meal was served by the man of the house, and frequently the ladies and children waited in another room, while the guests dined. The meal began by a 10 minute opening prayer with each of us standing around the table. It was not the custom to serve a beverage with the meal. On those cases when water was provided with the meal, it generally was one bottle set in the middle of the table from which everyone drank. The food was usually simply one course consisting of a peasant soup called Chorba or perhaps a second course of Mamaliga, a cornmeal mush poured onto a platter that set up with the consistency of stiff mashed potatoes. Occasionally, fried eggs accompanied the meal, and pieces of a white milky cheese. Food was scarce, and every morsel was deeply appreciated. At the end of the meal, all of those present again surrounded the table standing and saying a prayer. When departing a home, the family again gathered on their knees in the major room and prayed for your safe journey and quick return. The Pentecostals of Romania clearly were a devout and grateful people who truly lived in respect and awe of God. Communism and its persecution of the faithful had birthed a deep spiritual understanding and awareness of God that drew me to these people. I felt privileged and blessed beyond my wildest dreams to be sharing prayers, meals and love with these believers.

In the morning, we sorted through clothing and food, arranging things in plastic bags for families. Loading up the two vehicles, we headed out for the villages. The first village we visited was called Marganitta. About an hour's drive from town, we entered a small village of dirt roads and small wooden houses. There were a few sheep, and the occasional cow but for the most part the people appear to be out working in the fields. The houses were in disrepair, and the living conditions were horrific. Most houses had only two rooms, one with a table for eating and then another small room with a platform covering most of the floor space on which the entire family slept. Many of the families had 12, 13 and 14 children. We found a few families with as many as 20 children, some with obvious genetic defects. Downs syndrome was present in nearly every village and many people of all ages were malnourished. The adults were no better off than the children. Clothing in the houses was kept in cardboard or wood boxes. Most of the cooking was done outdoors on a campfire. The only decoration in the house was usually a photo of a family member affixed to the wall with a small cloth draped across the top like a cornice. Many of the houses had broken windows or no windows. Some houses had an outhouse and others did not even have that convenience. Water was carried from nearby wells in plastic buckets and washing was done at the riverside, a well, or in an irrigation ditch. We opened the trunk lid and started passing out clothing and food. When we found someone who had reading skills we would hand them the Bible. Before long we had people running towards us from all over the fields, many yelling "Biblia, Biblia", meaning Bible. They desired the clothing and the food, but most of all they wanted that precious Bible.

One elderly woman approached me and I gave her small bar of Ivory soap. She smelled it over and over, and then held it close to her chest. Where ever we went in the village the rest of the afternoon, I noticed she was walking behind us and saying something. I asked Vladimir what she was doing and he said she was praying blessings upon me for the gift. She was reciting Psalms and asking the Lord special favors upon me for this gift!

Once we were out of supplies in the cars, we started visiting families to pray with them. In one home, the lady asked us to come in and pray for her husband, who could not walk. We found him laying on a clay platform carved out of the wall in the second room of the sod house. As we anointed him with oil and prayed for him, the lady prepared a small lunch for us. When we came out from the room, she had set her small table with six bowls. In each bowl, she had placed a small fish about the size of a herring and covered it with sprigs of grass and a little milk from a cow. We ate standing, as there were no chairs, and only one stool. It was difficult but necessary that we accept her offering she had graciously prepared for us. With bread, we were able to eat most of the fish. Fortunately, this was two years before I developed my seafood allergy. It was very important to her that she provide a gift of food and this was all she had to offer.

At the next house, I noticed an unusual leather harness hanging on the wall. I asked what it was for. The lady said it was used for her sister. Then she went and got her sister, a lady of about 50 years of age, who was hunched over and blind. She demonstrated how they would put the harness upon the sister with a lead line in front and then they would strap things to her back and use her to pack things back and forth from the fields. I was appalled to realize this lady was being used as a pack animal. I asked Vladimir about this and he said under Ceausescu you had to be of use in order to get food. The state simply would not permit people to not contribute in some way whether sightless or not. If you did not work you were placed in prison, or worse. When we went back to the farmhouse that evening, I was in shock at what I had seen. In all of my travels I had never met people living in such deplorable conditions as these Romanian peasants. I went to my room and got on the floor and prayed. I told the Lord indeed I would be His hands and His feet, and I would serve him in Romania. I knew my life had changed forever that day. As I prayed through the night, the Lord gave me visions of the wealth of America and the waste in our lives that should be shared with the rest of the world. He reminded me of Caleb, the lieutenant of Joshua in the Old Testament, and how he went forth to survey the land and report back. I decided I would form a ministry called Caleb and its avowed purpose would be to do love gifts unto others in the name of Jesus, without reward. I cried through the night. I knew my life would never be the same.

The next morning, with the two vehicles again loaded with clothing and food and Bibles, we drove three hours south to the District Petrican. We visited another village called Neamt. The roads were hostile to vehicles, obviously having been used primarily by livestock, and horse-drawn carts, and the occasional tractor. Before the day was done, we managed to break the axle on one of our vehicles! Neamt is a small village nestled in the hills of central Romania, remote from large towns and urban influence. The local people herd sheep, make cheese, carve wood from Cottonwood trees, and farm. Packing up sacks of clothing and food, we again found great enthusiasm for copies of the Bible from the local people. They were in the process of building a church on land donated by a local pig farmer, adjacent to his livestock pen. The walls had been framed and a top and adequate concrete block foundation, but they had no money to finish the building and provide the roof necessary to protect it from the harsh winter. Taking a collection amongst ourselves, we raised $379 and gave it to the pastor to purchase supplies for the roof. The next day, we saw him in Suceavea on his horse-drawn cart buying the wood for the roof.

Walking through the village, we were offered samples of the local cheese and water drawn from the wells, for refreshment. The locals were very curious about us and how we got to their town. A stream accompanied the road through the village, and there was the occasional log crossing the stream serving as a bridge or walkway. Deep into the village, a peasant man approached and grabbed me by the arm and led me across the log to his house. He had received a sack of clothing and food and he wanted to show me his family. With no choice, I went along climbing the hill. On top, we reached a simple concrete block building with portals prepared for windows and doors and a small garden outside. About half had a roof as it was under construction, apparently as he obtained supplies to go forward. He had a few geese and a horse, shared with several neighbor families. Coming into the shell of a house, he introduced us to his wife and three children, and beckoned us to stay for a minute. We stood and visited as there was no place to sit except two stumps or a stack of brinks. Blankets were on the floor where they obviously slept during the night and a small campfire was outside the doorway. He returned in a few minutes with a small candy dish, chipped and fractured but obviously cherished as "the best china" of this family. Inside the dish, there were approximately a dozen freshly picked raspberries, still ripening, from his garden. He offered them to us as a gracious host, the only thing he had to give unexpected guests. We each took a raspberry and ate, ignoring the green, and we exchanged names and addresses. I was now a part of the family of Vasile Arhile! We were brothers. This was the beginning of a friendship that has endured nearly 20 years. This simple peasant man had appropriated me into his family. Anything he had was mine to use or take, without hesitation. He looked after me like a guardian angel, walking in front to clear the path or remove brush or limbs, serving me food, brushing my clothes, or providing a cup of water from the well. In his way, he was the ideal host, wanting to serve as his humble means permitted!

Walking through the rest of the village, Vasile served as my guide and introduced me to many people, hanging onto my arm at all times. When it came to crossing the log to return to the roadway, he jumped into the river and waded across, holding my hand to steady me so that I did not get wet or fall in to the river! It was embarrassing, humiliating and yet comforting and gracious at the same time. I felt so unworthy of his consuming attention and yet understood it was something he felt the need to do for me.

We provided medicines and vitamins for many of the children in the village and held a small service in an open field before leaving. Returning to the Suceavea farmhouse, I once again spent the evening on the floor praying to God to make me his instrument in serving these forgotten people. I cried through the night and received repeated visions and prophecies forming the basis of a new ministry. The Lord gave me visions of airplanes flying from Seattle to Eastern Europe, filled with medicines and medical supplies. He showed me pallets of foods, bundles of clothing, and boxes and boxes of books, all being passed out among the people in the small villages of Eastern Europe, not just Romania. After each addition, I claimed it in the name of Jesus and promised the Lord I would do everything I could to have it come true. I was cautioned by His word that no one was to profit; all of the goods were to be used in His glory for His people. The name Caleb had already been used by me in describing our men's Fellowship program at home. For me, it signified one who seeks out the needs of others and then works to fulfill them, **to the glory of God**. It was the perfect name for this new ministry to Eastern Europe. We had become the Lieutenant in Joshua's army, The ARMY OF GOD!

In the coming days, we visited many similar villages and preached in many towns. The people always welcomed us. They offered what ever they had, and they invited us into their families without hesitation. They were curious about our church, our families and the reason why we journeyed so far across the world to provide them with help. The only answer I had was that I was led by God. One morning we met with a lady who had been beaten and sent away by her husband with their three children, because she had accepted Jesus as her savior. He was Muslim. We provided her with a stipend to obtain an apartment, clothing for her children and herself and food for her family. Introducing her to a local pastor, she was taken under their wing without hesitation. Romania had suffered much at the hands of ruthless leaders. The ancient thinking of macho nature of the man still dominated the culture. And coupled with influences of atheism and Muslim thinking, most women were powerless. They were viewed as property or tools without legal standing. Church influence had been minimized by the official atheism. It was easier for a Dictator to keep control when he only had to deal with men so keeping the women insignificant helped their cause.

Under the communist dictatorship of Nikolai Ceausescu, Romania was an atheist country and all who profess a belief in God were labeled fools. Yet, the totalitarian regime left intact the Romanian Orthodox Church and the many monasteries throughout the land, as historical treasures they dare not touch. Technically, all Romanians were born as members of the Orthodox Church. But under communism it had waned into an insignificant oddity. Pentecostalism, and Protestant worship were basically an underground movement within the country. Any church was viewed as a potential threat to the communist regime. To possess a Bible subjected you to 75 days in jail. A pastor or clergy, who did not spy for the regime, would be imprisoned for up to 14 years in the most miserable of conditions. Many clergy were in prisons when the revolution occurred and we were privileged to be there as they were released and returned to their home villages and towns. It was with these persecuted pastors and priests that we were now holding services of rebirth of the faith across the lands. It was a privilege and an awesome experience to meet with and pray with and serve with these brothers and sisters in Christ. The avowed first purpose of Caleb Ministries became the empowering and encouraging of these servants of God as they returned to their communities. To rebuild the church and empower its servants was our calling!

As we traveled back across Romania we visited several large towns and preached in the local churches, some previously underground churches secreted in basements, and hidden rooms. It seemed strange to me that people in various areas referred to Vladimir by different names. In one community, he was known as Joseph and in other they called him Luke. In Constanta, he was addressed as Robert and in Moldova they used his Russian name Vladimir. (He was born in the Russian section of Romania, and therefore given a Russian name at birth, though of a Romanian family) He explained that years ago when he escaped from Romania under Ceausescu, he fled to the west and established an underground program for continuing to serve the church in Romania. He had to flee his homeland, because he and his wife were apprehended, teaching the Bible to children. His current home church in Frankfurt, Germany, provided him with a living, and there they collected clothing and food and Bibles to be smuggled back into the homeland. He did two weekly radio programs on Iberian radio, beamed directly into Romania not unlike Voice of America broadcasts. Also a weekly children's radio program was broadcast by him on Iberian radio. The broadcast waves came directly across the Mediterranean Sea, reaching most of Romania and Moldova and Bulgaria! He frequently came into the country under disguise, often making people aware he was coming by messages hidden in his radio broadcasts. The various identities and names were for his own protection, making it difficult for the authorities to track him. He published a book detailing some of these ventures, called "The Book They Could Not Ban" by Vladimir Caravan.

Though Pastor Lawrence was not comfortable with the rigors of travel in less than secure conditions and rudimentary comforts, I purposed myself to return to Romania as frequently as the Lord would permit. The absence of hygiene or privacy or modern conveniences did not sway me for a second. I could not get enough of being with these people of God so reliant and so faithful in the face of certain persecution.

By the time I had returned to Seattle, I had changed within and I knew my life would never be the same. Discussing the situation with my wife, she understood my need to return and serve in the mission field. She consented to my plan as long as she did not have to come with me. I immediately put my law office up for sale and retired from the active practice of law, dedicating myself to the development of Caleb Ministries. Applying for incorporation with the state of Washington and recognition through IRS as a 501(c)3 nonprofit organization, I began to seek people for an advisory board. Many came forward from my prayer groups and people in my church. People became very supportive. Caleb Good News Ministries was founded.

# Chapter 12

# Return To The Mission Field

*Josh 24:15*

*15 And if it seem evil unto you to serve the Lord, choose you this day whom ye will serve; whether the gods which your fathers served that were on the other side of the flood, or the gods of the Amorites, in whose land ye dwell: but as for me and my house, we will serve the Lord.*
*KJV*

In my first journey to Romania I desired to bless the Lord by serving him and his believers in the Third World. On my second trip, I learned the Lord wanted to bless me by permitting me to serve him through his resources throughout the entire world. What an eye-opener this was for me!

My second journey to Romania was in just a month after the first, Vladimir, brother George and I drove from Frankfurt to the Romanian border, once again. This time we went to the city of Arad on our entry and then to Timisoara where we picked up Pastor Ianos Nikolai. I was privileged to meet some of the pastors responsible for the prayer meetings that initially sparked the revolution in Romania. What a wonderful opportunity this was! In the evening we preached in a college setting with many young people present. Vladimir was becoming more comfortable with my message and accepting of me. Ianos Nikolai became a very good friend and sponsor, introducing me to many important people of the revolution as well as inviting me into his family. Both men were very pleased with the medicines and supplies I brought from America on my second trip in 16 duffel bags. We began to gel as a team and by the time we reached Suceavea the three of us were joined by a Russian evangelists named Sergei and the District Director of the Pentecostal Union in Suceavea. We rented a hall and conducted evangelism on four nights. Ianos and I preached the first hour with the Vladimir translating for me and Vladimir and Sergei the second hour. An intermission was filled with worship time utilizing several Pentecostal church choirs from Suceavea. There was great response each evening, but we kept hearing disturbing reports of people being beaten up by the police on their way home after our meetings. We decided to stop the evangelism and concentrate on speaking in churches so people did not get hurt. The Securitate secret police of Nicholas Ceausescu was still doing its work in intimidating and bullying Christians despite the assassination of their leader. What the West did not understand about Romania, was that the removal of Ceausescu as dictator did not remove his followers from power, who still harbored communist beliefs and great resentment towards the West. There was no other resource in place in Romania to govern the people. Those who had been in power changed their allegiance to a socialist philosophy, publicly, but continued to govern pretty much as before. They paid only lip service to reforms under the new presidency of the former vice president of Nicholas Ceausescu! Change was slow to come in Romania. Not only was the country deeply in debt and lacking resources, it lacked the will and desire to become a democracy at the top.

Most of those in positions of power resented our efforts to help those in need. There was clear animosity towards westerners; obstacles were raised continuously. We were threatened in back rooms, denied permits or access for petty reasons, and bullied at every opportunity. I recall going for a permit in one city and being taken by the clerk to an upper floor. Once we were inside the elevator with the door closed, it was made abundantly clear I would receive no cooperation or courtesy whatsoever. When the door opened, all was polite, courteous and hospitable. Later, that same official stood next to me in church pledging his support and gratitude for the public and church goers! But I knew we would eventually prevail no matter what they did to try to stop us. The Lord was on our side. I was for more angered than intimidated! Clearly, Suceavea would not make a good center for our ministry.

In the mountains of Transylvania in southwestern Romania, we came to the mining town of Petrosani. It was here that Caleb Ministries established its first big headquarters in Eastern Europe. Our first visit with Vladimir Caravan introduced me to Pastor Ile Trian. The father of 12 children, including a Down's Syndrome daughter, Adriana, Ile's church became a favorite stop of mine. Pastor Ile led the Emmanuel Pentecostal Church in this rough mining town. The miners had been pampered under Nikolai Ceausescu. The dictator courted favor with them and they did his bidding in holding down unrest across Romania. When a crowd became unruly or street demonstrations began, Ceausescu would bring in trainloads of miners from Petrosani to discipline the demonstrators. In exchange, miners were granted higher wages than others, better housing at state expense, and longer vacations. This favoritism slowly ceased with the assassination of the totalitarian leader but bringing the mining community into

respectable status with the rest of the Romanians and introducing these hard working people to the love and service
commanded by Jesus became a formidable task. Pastor Ile
was up to the challenge! His character was above reproach,
and his teachings squarely rooted in God's Word.

His entire family worked as a unit in leading the community into Christ-likeness. Petrosani was opening itself to the
rest of the country. Plans were underway to build a new
church on the hillside overlooking the entire mining valley.
No longer feared among the rest of the country, his church
became an example to other communities on living in
harmony and maturing in their walk. He built more churches,
reached out to poor communities, shepherded people previously left to their own devices, and started a disciplined
Seminary and music ministries. Pastor Ile was rallying the
forces and leading the charge bringing Romania into the
world community.

Visiting with the family in their small house situated in
the old poorer section of town known as the colony, the hospitality was incomparable. We held many table discussions and
free exchanges of ideas, and it was clear from our first meetings that Pastor Ile Trian and his church and Caleb Ministries
would be doing joint programs. Once the land was secure
for construction of a new big church, we were privileged to
share by providing dental equipment for a free dental bureau,
furnishing materials and furniture for four Sunday school
classrooms, equipment to service a garage, and supplies for
an apartment for visiting pastors and their guests. A church
in Sweden provided financing and materials for the bulk of
the sanctuary and building and Caleb Ministries was privileged to be part of the workforce in making bricks, sending
books and texts for a library, and preparing the foundations of
construction. When finished, the Filadelphia church housed
the first Caleb warehouse in Romania, a garage for storing
the Caleb vehicles, and a library supplied by books from

Seattle. The Filadelphia church in Petrosani has over 1000 members today, has 14 satellite churches, a Bible college, and a Christian school and is sending missionaries into other parts of the world. In 1995 Caleb was privileged to provide supplies for the opening of a free medical clinic operated by the church and situated in a nearby apartment building. The dental clinic continues to give free dental service as well. Church services are broadcast across western Romania via radio and the Church hosts conferences and fellowship gatherings throughout the region.

On one subsequent visit I was provided a young man to interpret as I preached. When I finished, he asked Pastor Ile if he could give a brief testimony. He stated those three years previous, he was housed at an orphanage at Vulcan where Caleb had visited. We gave him a walkman and cassettes of Bible Teachings at the orphanage and he was led to Christ. He then promised God he would learn English to serve as a translator for me, which he did! Caleb gave away hundreds of such walkmans with cassettes of teachings and songs in Romanian.

Journeying down to Constanta, the port city for Romania on the Black Sea, we were introduced to the most prosperous city in Romania, where during communism most high government officials and members of the secret police lived in opulence during the totalitarian years. The city had many gypsies, and many poor but also signs of prosperity unusual to the rest of the country. Separated from the mainland by the Danube River and a canal hand excavated by forced labor years before, special taxes and tolls were charged to enter into this privileged area. Constanta incurred no uprising during the revolution and was mostly untouched by the Civil War that raged throughout the rest of the country. Here we met a very courageous pastor and had the immense honor to conduct services in his underground church. Now six months since the revolution, many Romanians still expected their country to return to the Soviet bloc. The Russians had had so much influence over this country for 46 years that The Soviet Union was still viewed as the world power with whom their fate was cast. Because the United States had never intervened in the Hungarian Revolution or the uprisings in Czechoslovakia and Poland, people in the eastern bloc believed their future lay only under Russian influence! They feared, but fully expected a return to totalitarian rule, and did not easily expose their faith to others. Most church members kept to themselves about their faith, and it was very difficult to get any Romanians except pastors, who accepted persecution, to publicly declare themselves as believers in Christ.

It became a primary emphasis of Caleb ministries to encourage the public declaration of faith and to help establish open Christian churches throughout the land. Most Christian groups met in secret in small houses or apartments, late at night. There was great risk, seen by locals in bringing anyone new into the fellowship. The Holy Spirit was heavy, wherever we were met but a spirit of fear gripped many locals. Once they trusted us, those who prayed openly prayed with fervor like I had never seen before. It is for this reason, we witnessed many healings, many words of prophecy, and visions and miraculous events. People who have little of anything can only depend upon the Lord. When all hope was taken away, there was Jesus.

Even in Constanta, there were signs of the decay and neglect in the foundations of society. Most apartment houses and institutions were in very poor condition. Paranoia permeated the people. We learned from several sources of the artificial lake, constructed near Constanta by the Army in the 1980s'. Young boys 14 and 15 years of age were conscripted, whose families did not belong to the Communist Party. They had been ordered to build an earthen dam across the artificial lake not knowing the water in the lake was intentionally made radio active. The Army then did testing to see how long a soldier might survive in the battlefield during a radioactive attack. This human experimentation was then sold to other Soviet states. This exploitation was used as a form of raising capital for the Romanian government. This kind of cruelty was commonplace in the eastern bloc countries and accepted by those in authority. You can imagine for yourself how now these people felt after years of sacrifice and despair to have gifts of love and comfort from American Christians brought halfway around the world. Our offerings of chocolate bars, toys for the children, Bibles in Romanian, aspirin and tooth-paste, clothing, cheese and meat loaves, and preaching of God's love gave them renewed hope.

On my third journey, in Constanta, we rented the Nicolai Ceausescu Hall for $30 a night and conducted evangelism utilizing Vladimir, Ianos and myself. Four young ladies from Calvary Chapel in California came to help by providing worship music. We drew substantial crowds, posted notices of the meetings throughout Constanta. There was no repeat of the violence suffered in Suceavea. With the help of an Italian ministry, we held tent revivals from Cluj to Oradea! It was exciting to see the Word received with enthusiasm and to begin to see local Pastors becoming confident to publicly preach Gods word.

Traveling across Romania, I became accustomed to the control towers erected at every major road intersection. It was here that drivers had to submit their documents to show they had permission to travel from one city to the next during the communist era. With the revolution, most of the police were in hiding now that the government had been over-thrown. Having made a good living through extortion and rampant corruption for years, members of law enforcement deemed it wise to keep a low profile and the control towers were mostly unmanned. In many cities, the electrical system and steam heating plants were in bad repair, making public services undependable or even unavailable. We became used to non-functioning traffic lights and the absence of water and heat most everywhere we went. The locals were finding bread and cheese and rice available by waiting in long lines. If one were willing to stand in a queue, you could get groceries but no selection. Coffee was very difficult to find but packages of noodles and rice from Vietnam were plentiful in the north. One large grocery store in Suceavea that I visited had only pig's feet, Vietnamese noodles and jars of canned fruits and vegetables well beyond the expiration date for sale. But petroleum for car in the larger cities was a different matter as literally hundreds of cars sat in parking lots covered with dust and parked. The average Romanian who owned a private vehicle could not afford to drive it. Nor could they get permits to travel within the country. Cars that were being used were in disrepair. You always took your windshield wipers with you or locked them in the glove box when you left your car. Vandals would often throw stones or bricks through the windshields of moving cars and then take the victims belongings when they were disoriented by the crash. This was a country without police protection, or comforts. One dared not venture out alone.

On my fifth journey to Romania I entered with Vladimir through the city of Oradea and met a new friend Aron Filimon. He was a musician and worked with youth as well as having a band that played for church, weddings and social locations. His wife and children became my hosts on many later journeys. I recall, on one occasion when Vladimir journeyed off to parts unknown, Aron took me to a large pavilion where I had the privilege of addressing a crowd of several hundred teenagers. They were obviously intrigued to hear about America. Aron's band played and it became quite the happening. Several other churches contacted us, and I found many new friends in Oradea. One church eventually provided me with an apartment where I could stay whenever I came to their town without charge.

We went to Bucharest, where I met Vladimirs brother
and sister, and other members of the family. In the effort to
attempt to capture Vladimir, the Securitate secret police had,
years before, erected a tower within clear view of his sisters
house and another overseeing his brother's apartment. As a
consequence, the family ventured out from Bucharest to see
Vladimir on his visits or met with him in the underground
subway station. His sister was a delightful host, and I stayed
with her in her quaint two room house on numerous occasions
even after I stopped traveling with Vladimir. The brother and
his wife remain my good friend to this day. When their son
became a target of the Securitate secret police for having
participated in the revolution, we helped him and his wife to
leave the country and find safe haven in Canada. This came
about one day, when the son discovered his college school
records had been expunged and his identity card was suddenly
no longer on file at the municipal building, indicating he was
a non-person. He had been involved in the campus uprisings against Ceausescu and now the police were reviewing
video to identify and punish those involved. Once we had
helped "arrange" their escape, we contacted friends in the
Canadian and Australian embassies to provide safe asylum
in Hungary. The Canadians responded first, and they were
eventually relocated in Vancouver, British Columbia. Caleb
volunteers then provided them with household furnishings
and food and visited them frequently. They reciprocated by
then translating documents for us, helping others who immigrated to Canada and the United States from the Eastern
Bloc, and by reading Bible stories in Romanian onto our
cassettes, which we then distributed in Romania.

On another journey to Romania in 1990, Vladimir had
asked that I obtain four visas for travel to the country of
Moldova from the Moldovan Consulate in the United States.
Moldova is the eastern portion of Romania, severed at the
end of WWII and awarded as a political plum to the Russian

influence. As a puppet government of Moscow, all ties were broken between Romania, and its former Eastern District. The Moldovans and Romanians played diplomatic games with both sides during the cold war but Moldova eventually became a strict and unwavering supporter of the Soviet bloc. Russian was the imposed language and all travel between the two countries was discouraged by those governing the Moldovans. A wall was eventually erected very similar to the Berlin wall, cutting off families from each other. The Moldovan Barrier was not torn down until1994, and even then travel was strictly regulated by Moldova.

Vladimir stated he wanted to take the district director of churches in Suceavea, brother George from Nuremberg, and myself into Moldova in 1990 but as a Romanian he could not secure the necessary passports. After several efforts, I obtained the four visas through the consulate office in San Francisco and gave them to Vladimir.

But when we arrived in Suceavea, we were met by a friend of his from Germany who also wanted to go to Moldova. He decided that I would remain in Suceavea in the farmhouse, while the rest of them journeyed across the border using the four visas I had obtained from the San Francisco consulate. This was a huge disappointment to me but I accepted it as I was there to serve Vladimir and I understood his desire to bless his longtime friends who helped financed his ministry. A further hurt occurred when Vladimir told me I was to wait for him in the farm room until he returned. To add further insult, he asked me to spend my time re-labeling 1200 Romanian Bibles that my church had purchased with the inscription on the title page "gift from -omitted name- Church". In fact, Caleb ministries had raised the money for the Bibles, with the express intent that they be given anonymously to Romanians, as is always the custom in our ministry. He resold them to another church and wanted me to assist by inserting their name as the donor! All of the items that Caleb Ministries has provided throughout the world have never born the name Caleb Ministries, except only as required by customs and importation laws. They are only represented as a gift from Jesus!

However, I knew that Vladimir had sold the Bibles to the Colorado church and was using the money he received to support his family. I did not approve, but was not asked my opinion so I did as he wished.

He left with his friends for Moldova on Monday morning. I had no one to talk to and was faced with four days of being alone except for having a plate of food brought in twice a day. The pastor's wife was very busy looking after the seven children who lived in their adjoining house and she did not speak English. Finishing my assignment of taping labels into the Bibles, I did my devotions, and then walked up into town. There, I met a Mennonite gentleman, who spoke perfect English. He asked what I was doing in Suceavea, and I told him a little bit about myself. He asked if I wanted to go to church with him tonight and I said yes. He picked me up at 5 p.m. and took me to a large Pentecostal Church where he introduced me to the pastor and then interpreted for me while I preached! Then he took me to a second church, and I preached again. The next morning he arrived early, bringing me my breakfast, and having two companions with him. We drove out to surrounding towns and met several pastors and preached the word. On the third afternoon, he took me to his home, where I was fed lunch and we visited with his friends and family. Then we went to Botosani, a larger town to the east, and onto Iasi, the ancient capitol of eastern Romania and second largest city in Romania. In sum, the four days that Vladimir was gone, were very productive in not only giving me great opportunity to preach but letting me appreciate that I could travel on my own in missions. The Lord clearly would provide and I had nothing to fear in going without Vladimir.

When the four returned from their trip to Moldova, they heard from people throughout the town how the Mennonites had taken me to several churches. For their part, the trip to Moldova was very unsuccessful as the Moldovan government never let them in, refusing to honor the visas issued in my name without me. They were forced to wait 14 hours at the border and then turned away. They returned in the second day, and waited another 12 hours, but again were denied entry. It appears the visas required that I accompanied the group in order for them to be valid since they were issued to me as a US citizen.

From then on Vladimir and I spoke openly about the possibility of duel ministries in the coming year and he was comfortable with that, though he wanted to continue to receive the medical supplies we were sending. I assured him that would be no problem. He presented me with a map of Romania as a gift for launching my individual travels. I used that map, as there were few maps of Romania or Moldova available. Then in 1994 a lady in Bucharest broke out laughing, telling me the map Vladimir gave me was a map of the railroads and not the highways!

In December, I received another call from Vladimir asking me to come and help him driving a semi-truck and trailer of toys into Romania from Holland, a donation from a Dutch toy factory. This was a quick journey as it was winter travel and our mission was very specific in getting the toys to orphanages in Cluj, Bistritsa, Suceavea, Iasi, Roman, Constanta, Bucharest, Craiova and Timisoara. We visited orphanages in each city, where I saw for myself the deplorable conditions facing these children and the staffs. In truth, most of the children in "orphanages" were not orphans. They either were children who were wards of the state because of handicaps or impairments or illness, or they were children given over to the state to raise because the families were unable to care for them at that time. Romania takes the position children are property of the state and not of a family. Even today, when a child is approximately 3 months of age, the state intervenes to see if the living conditions are appropriate. They provide a stipend to the family for care of each child, and they assign a government agency to oversee the children in their growing years. Each year, every child in Romania is required to be relinquished to the government for a one-month summer camp, where the children are instructed by the government and where they are observed for any deficiencies in their upbringing.

Under the teaching of the Romanian Orthodox Church, instruction was given that a woman must bear children as long as she is physically capable. To fail to do so is considered a sin and a risk of loss of her salvation. The passage in 1st Timothy chapter 2 verse 15 translates that a woman's salvation shall be by childbirth. This interpretation resulted historically in large families for church members. Though hardly a religious zealot, dictator Nicolai Ceausescu seized upon this situation to build his cheap labor force as an asset for Romania to market to the Soviet bloc. He encouraged large families as well, dove-tailing into the teachings of the Romanian Orthodox Church. The state rewarded the larger families by offering tax breaks and incentives. Being an agricultural society, and one that suffered historically from genocide, and attrition by poor health and disease, the Romanians readily accepted these teachings and incentives, and it was not unusual for a family to have 15, 16 or 17 children. We have found families of 23 and 24 children even this day in villages. One family we support in Dorohoi has 26 children! The teaching of abortion or birth control is rigorously opposed by the church and the government.

Because families could not feed or provide care for so many children, the state expanded its system of orphanages to permit any family to leave children with the state schools without expense and even to regain the children into their family when the older ones left or the family had increased means to support them all. This resulted in a system of literally hundreds of orphanages throughout the country, many with very poor living conditions and all drastically under-staffed. When the borders opened with the Revolution in 1990, Westerners were appalled to view what they deemed so many orphans and to see the deplorable living conditions in the state institutions. Adoptions were rampant and because of the money offered by Westerners to procure children, many administrators and staff in institutions permitted adoptions of orphans, who were not true orphans. Even sick children whose medical records had been falsified, were adopted. It was not uncommon for a well-meaning Westerner to arrive in Romania offering $5,000 to $10,000 for an adoption when the national standard of living brought an annual income of less than $500. The temptation was great and the consequences chaotic. Eventually it became inevitable for the Romanian government to stop all adoptions in order to sort out children who had been misidentified as orphans, and to prosecute those who were making a lucrative living from fraud. To make matters even worse, French, British and American television networks broadcast pictures and videos showing the shocking and unspeakable living conditions in a few of the poorer state institutions. Many children were malnourished, unclothed, battered and living in hideous situations. Not since the Holocaust, has there been such an outcry against a populace as rose against the Romanians in the western world. Understandably, the Romanian government then turned decidedly against foreign adoptions and ceased visits to state institutions by foreigners. It became necessary to have a police escort when visiting any institution within Romania and the taking of photographs was expressly prohibited.

It was in this atmosphere that Vladimir and I were passing out toys and games to children in orphanages across the land. To gain entry into the institutions we had to engage in gifts of medicines and vitamins for the children and make assurances that we in no way encouraged or assisted anyone in adoption proceedings. This was a difficult sell for me in that my passport listed me as a practicing attorney from the United States, but we managed to convince them of my good intentions.

In 1992, I again returned to Romania with Vladimir Caravan in February. On this occasion, we made our first visit together to the town of Braila on the Danube River in south- eastern Romania. This visit was to become of monumental importance to Caleb ministries in future years. Arriving about four in the afternoon on a cold wintry day, we were welcomed in a farmhouse situated in the center of the city. Surrounded by apartment houses and commercial buildings, the tiny farm sported a garden, a stable with a cow, horse, chickens, and pigs. It was clear the farm's future was in grave doubt with the town encroaching n all sides, but the family remained untroubled. Upon our arrival, I was led to a bedroom and told to sleep. It was not unusual for me to be given abrupt instructions such as this because our language skills were not that well developed. Knowing I was told to "take a nap" for good reason, I obliged without question. About nine o'clock in the evening I was awakened and invited to eat some soup and bread. Then I was led across the muddy backyard to what we might call a bunkhouse on an American farm. Here there were two small rooms and a small porch. Each room had a platform that served as a bed that covered approximately half of the floor space. It consisted of a plywood platform covered with blankets and an occasional pillow. However, the room was now full of people singing and praying. Around the edge of the wall was a bench and in the floor space there were small stools and crates to sit on. Every inch of the floor and bed-platform was occupied by people. They had saved one chair against the back wall next to the ceramic fireplace for me. I was at my first "long night service". The celebration known as "the long night" came about in response to persecution under communism. To hide their identity as believers but still fellowship together, worship God, and learn scripture, the Pentecostal Churches would hold a service once a month at a home, farm, workplace, or even an apartment, passing on the information to others in strict confidence. On the appointed evening, each believer would come to the designated location after work, staying until morning or dawn, when their departure would appear to be normal for going to work or the fields. The service began at nine thirty or ten p.m. with singing, praying, and messages from pastors or elders. The pattern would be repeated throughout the evening and early morning hours. Usually about 1 or 2 a.m., a plate of bread and cheese or sliced green peppers or small cakes would be passed around. The ladies would sit mostly on the bed, some knitting or sewing, mending, kneading bread or otherwise working because ancient scripture says the ladies worked through the night at Dorcas' house! Prayer through the evening was by everyone getting on their knees, crowded together in the tiny floor space! Coming to the service, one brought a basket or box if they had something to share such as squash, melons, apples, bread, mushrooms or other goods. The elders divided the items brought among all the baskets and boxes on the porch during the night so that everyone got a share to take home in the morning. This church service was modeled on the Book of Acts and Agape Love in its purest form. The church held everything in community as a family. If anyone had a need, it was expressed, discussed and addressed. They saw that all had work or chores, each family had food, and no one was left unattended or in need!

At my first long night service they had me talk and preach and teach repeatedly through the night, being very curious to learn about the western church and our ministry.

This was a very informal setting with questions and ideas presented in conversational manner. They were quite interested in my experiences in prison ministry and in working with aids patients, in how I selected my sermon topics and where I had preached. The Braila Church was headed up by Gheorge Streghor but used a Hungarian Pastor Kerkes Tibor as well. Teaching was done by several elders as well as the Pastors. They were very musical with a ministry leader who himself knew over 300 songs, composed many by himself, and played many instruments. To support itself, the church operated what they called "The Business". It consisted of all members of the church. They bid on jobs of all kinds such as remodeling factories, building houses and businesses, painting, moving, farming fields and gleaning crops, processing food, repair of machinery, printing, and maintaining livestock. Most everything was owned in common by the church community and all was shared with others. When they got a new job, they always hired one unemployed non-believer to work alongside a believer so that the job became an evangelism tool. The church had a rented building in town were they held public services on Sunday Mornings but they never invited anyone to the "long night service" until they had attended Sundays for some time and had evidenced some gift of the Spirit.

The Braila Church helped me grow spiritually far more than I could have imagined. I immediately gravitated towards each and everyone, feeling acceptance and fellowship and kinship as never before. I was being healed of past hurts and offense as I worshipped in their meetings! The songs opened up scriptural truths and their life style demonstrated a love for one another. As they wanted to know about churches in America, I kept wishing the Western Church were more like theirs!

On my next trip, my visa was about to expire, and it became necessary for me to leave Romania for two days, after which I could re-enter and have a renewed 30 day visa. Ianos and Vladimir and I headed for Bulgaria because the western border crossings were still clogged and painfully slow. Once in Bulgaria, we visited Sofia. slept in the car that night and then decided to head south to the port city of Bourgas where Vladimir had some friends to visit. We arrived about 4 in the afternoon and visited the apartment of his friend, a Russian, now living in Bulgaria. The gentleman was elderly and scholarly having authored many books as well as a Bible concordance, all in Russian. His writings were why he could no longer live in his home country. He showed me how he wrote manuscripts, gave them to Vladimir and they were then spirited out of Bulgaria and Romania across to the West where they were then published and circulated, being hidden in false compartments of two fender gas cans! He provided us with additional manuscripts on this trip to return to Germany. He had been imprisoned in Russia in his earlier years for his writings but there was no law in Bulgaria against his writing Russian language books, though he was watched by the authorities.

Following a dinner of tomato slices, black olives and cheese, we headed to the church. Our timing was miraculous as the service was packed, the local clergyman having just been released from prison and hosting his first week of services since ending 12 years of incarceration, according to Vladimir. As the program began, they asked me to preach since I was from America! I spoke in English which Vladimir translated to Romanian. Another Pastor then translated it into Russian and in turn the Priest translated it into Bulgarian! Four languages employed so everyone could understand. Vladimir gave the second message which required only three translations. The Bulgarians were very interested, not seeing many Americans at that time and not having many visitors in their country! Following the service, I visited with young people in the courtyard outside. Most were high school or college age. One young man had a deformed right hand . we visited for a while and he took my address information. Later, he wrote and asked for help with college expenses as the Bulgarian Government would not permit him to attend college at state expense because of his deformity. Caleb Ministries undertook sponsoring him for 5 years at $75/month. He became the first of many to receive Caleb sponsorship for schooling. Today, he is an architect in Sofia and the assistant youth leader in his church!

As I was visiting with the young people, the church Pastor came out with Vladimir and asked that I pray for one of the ladies inside, for a healing. I said sure and we went inside into a small side chapel at the front of the church. I anointed the elderly lady as she knelt before me and placed my hands on her head, praying in the Spirit. She started shouting loudly "Halleluiah, Halleluiah" and some Bulgarian words. Not having any idea what she was saying, I just kept praying. Suddenly, the outside door opened and the outer sanctuary was filled with people kneeling, waiting to be prayed for! I handed a vial of anointing oil to Vladimir and we worked our way through, praying for each. It was almost 2 am when we finished, people standing and testifying of their healings with tears pouring down their faces. Most in peasant garb, the ladies with scarves covering their heads, men trying to give us coins for payment which we refused. I was concerned I would run out of anointing oil before we finished but when I looked, my tiny vial of oil was still full though clearly I had anointed over a couple of hundred people!

Returning to the apartment, we were exhausted! The electric power was out but our hosts' wife set out a candle on the table and a plate of olives, cheese and a loaf of bread. The five of us fell asleep on the floor right there. People do not realize the energy you expend when praying for others. It is exhilarating to see the Holy Spirit touching lives and to be a small part of it by becoming a conduit but each time I anoint and pray for others my body seems to loose energy. In a crowd it becomes exhausting because I have no time to pray and restore myself, but I never deny anyone a request to pray for them! It is a privilege I do not take lightly.

Awaking about 11 am, we cleaned up and shaved (in candle light still), left gifts with our guest for the hospitality, and headed back to Romania. I generally leave loaves of cheese, meat and powdered milk for families plus $20.00 for a nights stay, coffee or tea, and chocolate bars if there are kids. This is extravagant but it is our desire to help the families and we know they often go without to provide for us. We never give anything until we leave as otherwise they invariably serve it back to us.

At the border of Romania upon our return, I was advised and cautioned by the police that I had been tried by a military tribunal in Suceavea and sentenced to seven years in prison for possession of the 25,000 Bibles and an additional three years for entry into a forbidden reserve (The leper village). This was in 1992. I am often reminded of it when I return to Romania but no one has stopped my entrance or travels to date.

We proceeded back to Bucharest and then on to a village near Bistritsa where we officiated at a christening in the underground church. This was very big celebration as it was the eleventh child for the family, the sign of having a complete family to shield against illness, accident or genocide, and that the child was a boy meant prosperity to the family in future years. The celebration consisted of street dances, plates of Salomé' (cabbage rolls or grape leaf rolls of rice, meat and spices), Mamaliga (cornmeal mush set up like mashed potatoes), green peppers, cheese, tomatoes, bread, small cakes, and orange pop! The dancing went long into the night with family banners adorning the streets and relatives coming from miles around. It was an honor to be invited to participate in such a family festivity, just like they had known me for years!

It was clear that Vladimir achieved his purpose in introducing two American pastors to his beloved Romania. He appreciated the preaching and lessons presented by Pastor Lawrence who became his obvious preference to accompany him but Pastor Lawrence did not feel called to the mission field nor was he comfortable in that setting. In a sense, Vladimir was stuck with me or no one. The result was an alliance of convenience rather than a close bond of friendship. I was learning as we traveled and he accommodated me because I was able to supply medicines, funds, clothing and resources for helping in Romania. But some choices Vladimir made did not sit well with me. I traveled with him on four trips through Romania in 1990, five in 1991 and two in 1992 because it was the only avenue I had available to serve in the mission field there. We were cordial but not going to be life-long friends. When others were around, I was often left alone or excluded in conversations and planning. I accepted this and concentrated on my bible studies, forging contacts and relationships within the field, and serving Vladimir as best I could. The difficulty was with his approach to selling goods including bibles as he needed to support his family and his journeys. Where he would look to the more lucrative road to travel, I would be interested in helping those most in need. He wanted to serve only the Pentecostal churches and their memberships whereas I would give freely to all in need. This disparity surfaced often on our trips and I longed to be free to make decisions without his heavy hand. In fairness, he had a young family to support whereas I enjoyed greater resources than he. Also, I came from a relatively secure background and he from third world refugee circumstances.

# Chapter 13

# Right People: Wrong Country

*Heb 12:1-3*

*12:1 Wherefore seeing we also are compassed about with so great a cloud of witnesses, let us lay aside every weight, and the sin which doth so easily beset us, and let us run with patience the race that is set before us,*

*2 Looking unto Jesus the author and finisher of our faith; who for the joy that was set before him endured the cross, despising the shame, and is set down at the right hand of the throne of God.*

*3 For consider him that endured such contradiction of sinners against himself, lest ye be wearied and faint in your minds.*

*KJV*

In June 1992, I took my last trip into Romania with Vladimir. We were joined by Ianos Nikolai as we drove across the country delivering 20,000 children's Bibles written in Romanian purchased by Caleb from The David C. Cooke foundation. The churches were not the only ones excited to receive the Bibles. We found teachers and educators enthusiastic to use them in their public school curriculum as tools for teaching reading and writing to the students. It was rare for them to have good text books, with clear print in the Romanian language for the students. One teacher in Constanta begged us to get her another 10,000 copies for use in the entire school system in Constanta province. What an irony that you can't even read the Bible in an American school, and yet the Romanian teachers were begging us for them.

Vladimir had heard that there was a back road we could take to reach the Ukraine. He wanted to meet with some pastors in that country to coordinate future visits. In winding through the farm roads towards the east, we located an orphanage, previously unknown to us. Near Dorohoi at Pulmera, we found a boys home of 205 boys and a staff of eight adults. The school was a large farm situated out in the country. The buildings were in grave disrepair. The children had no toys. Clothing was quite shabby. One of the teachers shared with us that they had very few school supplies and no medications in their infirmary. They were forgotten out there in the countryside and rarely received any help from the government. They farmed their own land for food and had several cows and some chickens. They expressed surprise as we told them of the changes in government in their own country!. We gave them several copies of the children's Bible, though Russian was their working language. The children were excited as we gave them what spare clothes we had in our vehicle. We vowed to return with more.

In 1992, on one of my first journeys to Romania without Vladimir, I determined to find the boys home near Dorohoi. In preparation for the trip, we contacted numerous toy manufacturers and clothing companies to arrange special gifts for the boys. Leaving from Seattle with 22 duffel bags filled with clothes and toys and medicines, Dean Clingman and Dennis Wilson and I flew to Vienna. Both were members of my prayer groups and longtime friends. From Vienna we hitched a ride to Romania with another ministry, driving a very large bus filled with Bibles. We slept the night in eastern Hungary atop the Bibles which were stacked in the bus to the windows. It was one of the coldest nights I have ever spent and I could barely move in the morning. At the border the Romanian customs refused to allow the other ministry to bring in the Bibles as they were still contraband in such a large quantity. However, they welcomed us to bring in our medicines and clothing and toys for the children. We told them we would not come in unless they permitted the Bibles as well. The other ministry transferred the Bibles to us as part of our cargo and after several hours of negotiations with the customs authorities, they relented and permitted us to come in with everything, including the Bibles. Once we arrived inside the country the Bibles were then returned to the other ministry at Oradea and they gifted us five thousand of their Bibles for our use. In Oradea, my friend Aron Filemon obtained a Mercedes step-van for our use.

Driving across Romania, Dean, Dennis and I slept in the van and made our own meals from bread and cheese and bottled water as there were no restaurants open for travelers at that time. Arriving at Suceavea, we found the District church director not at home. We slept that night in the small room in the farmhouse. The next morning, we unloaded all of the duffel bags into the back of a van with the toys on top. We then drove the additional 65 miles to the boys home. Driving into the middle of the play field, we opened the rear door of the van and pushed out the toys onto the field. There were brand new basket balls, baseballs, footballs, gloves, jump ropes, soccer balls and assorted other toys galore. With the help of two teachers, we selected new clothing for each of the children. Using permanent ink markers, we wrote the names of the children on their items so that the school would know who they belong to. That way each child owned their toys and clothes and not the institution as was their custom. The children knew they had received gifts themselves that could not be taken away should they leave the school for any reason. The custom in Romania was that everything belonged to the institution or the state. When one adopted a child, they had to bring clothing to the institution to pick up their child because even the diapers remained with the facility when a child left. We then went to the infirmary and loaded it with Pediacare products, medicines, Band-Aids and first aid supplies. The administrator, head teacher and police were overwhelmed and did not know what to think. This was one of the best days of my life! Continuing on from Dorohoi, Dean and Dennis and I journeyed down to Braila and spent a few days with the church there. We preached on several occasions and worked with members of the church in developing street ministry and evangelism. They tried to teach us the Romanian language. We had English lessons each day to help them as many Romanians realized at that time their business future lay with communication with people in the Western world. The older kids wanted to come back with us to America but this was not feasible nor desirable. We encouraged them to stay and help rebuild their country!

One evening while we were preaching in the church, our van was vandalized. We came out from the church to find the radio antenna broken off, the radio removed, both rear view mirrors torn off and two flattened tires. It was interesting to hear one of the Brailans' to immediately lay blame with unidentified "orthodox gypsies", a non sequitur.! The people from the church were heartbroken to see our van in disrepair and promised to put it in operating order for us in the morning. It was an old van but it was the transportation we had. We walked back to the farmhouse about 3 miles away and one of the members took the tractor and towed the van to the farmhouse. The next morning when I awoke, I was very surprised at the work they had already done. They had fashioned a new radio antenna though we still had no radio to put in the van. Both flattened tires were removed from the van and they said they would find new tires and we should just relax for the morning. Finding tires for a vehicle, other than a Romanian Dacia Car, was very difficult. The church members set out as search team and combed the town. Later they reported back there were two stores that had automobile tires that might work. The first was called "Betties Boutique". They took us in their Dacia car to Betties Boutique. In 1992, there were very few private stores of any kind operating for the public. Most people made their own goods or ordered from catalogs and waited weeks for the items to arrive, or, bought from co-ops and government shops limited to party members. Betties Boutique turned out to be a small wood frame building about the size of a newspaper shack. They offered for sale two-liter plastic bottles of Pepsi or American cola or orange cola, Marlboro cigarettes, lotto tickets, and nine used automobile tires. That was literally all they had in the store. The strangest "boutique" I have ever seen! None of the tires was near the correct size for our van. We thanked them and then went to the second store which had reportedly a stock of tires as well. The store neon sign said "VCR REPAIR & TV" but was actually a paint shop! I asked about the sign and was told it was the only one available and colorful and therefore installed and lighted. It was indeed the most colorful storefront on the block. They had many gallons of paint and ladders and brushes. And in the corner were stacked five used automobile tires. Two of the tires were close to the correct size and so we purchased them for five dollars each.

Returning to the farm, the family had prepared lunch for us and insisted we eat while they put the tires on the van. When we finished lunch, which consisted of green peppers, radishes, cheese, bread, penepe verde (watermelon the size of cantelopes), and hot tea... we came out and found our van ready. I was taken aback immediately. The church co-op had just purchased a new tractor for use by all of the church members and to rent out for income to the church. It was a major purchase and the pride of the congregation! The tractor indebted the church 17.5 million lei which they figured would take 20 years to pay off. ($43,000 US). The farmer and pastor stood next to the tractor with a blow torch in hand. They had removed two mirrors from their new tractor and welded them to the frame of our old van. I was amazed and in tears for this generous gift. I could not imagine such generosity and sacrifice to deface their new tractor for our old rented van! The tires were installed and the van thoroughly cleaned as best they could!

As we started to get into the van to leave, many of the church members arrived carrying penepe verde (small water melons the size of cantelopes) because we had enjoyed it so much at lunch. Loading ourselves in the van with about 20 watermelon and our belongings, we headed back across Romania towards the western border. Stopping at Bucharest for the night at Inasmuch Romania ministry, the next morning we continued out across the country in a heavy fog. Near Deva we were traveling on a narrow concrete roadway when suddenly our van stopped without explanation. It did not run out of gas or appear to have a mechanical problem, but it simply coasted to a stop at a curve in the road adjacent to a roadside picnic table. We had been traveling about 60 mph. Since it was getting dark, we decided to sleep for the night and check out the engine in the morning. Placing the watermelon outside of the van, we slept in our sleeping bags. The next morning when I awoke, I exited the van and saw about 15 elderly people coming towards us out of the fog. They pointed at the penepe verde and I immediately understood why the Lord had provided us with 20 watermelon in Braila as there was no way we could eat them or take them on the airplane at Vienna to the USA. We gladly gave them the watermelon and then opened the engine compartment. We could find absolutely nothing wrong with the engine in any way. Finally we decided to try to start the van and it turned over immediately. Befuddled, we decided perhaps it had overheated the night before.

We packed up our belongings and drove onto the road and around the curve where we found the road totally washed out. If we had continued on that road the night before at the speed we were going we most certainly would have been in a deep ravine and most likely all killed. There were no warning signs, traffic cones or cautions of any kind.

In 2008 I was in Deva and had the privilege of addressing the Pentecostal church there on a Sunday morning. I recounted our adventures with the van and many of them remembered the road having been washed out by a flash flood back in 1992. Since that road was rarely used, no one thought to place a barricade across it.

When we returned to Oradea with the van, the owner was not upset with the "modifications" and was grateful for our work on behalf of his country. One of our hosts arranged for a driver to take us from Romania to Vienna to catch our airplane ride home. We were somewhat surprised when he arrived driving a tiny Opel in which he had three other passengers as well heading west. But even more surprising was when we arrived at the Romanian border crossing, he floored the accelerator and ran the border rather than stopping at the gate! Heading west at about 95 miles per hour, we three English-speaking Americans were shocked as we bulleted across Hungary towards the Austria border! That was when I realized years of communism taught many Romanians to view authority figures and the government as something to avoid, ignore or plot around! I decided it best not to try to rent cars in Romania in the future.

Dean Clingman accompanied me on two journeys to Romania and Dennis Wilson three trips. For most Romania outreaches, after separating from traveling with Vladimir in the spring of 1992, I journeyed alone three or four times a year. Later I learned that in 1993 he was apprehended by members of the Securitate secret police while traveling alone in a rural area near Cluj, Romania. They took him, beat him severely, and left him for dead in a gully. He was found the next morning by a farmer where he was recognized by friends. From there they got him to Germany. He has no recollection of the attack that occurred, having suffered severe brain damage. I visited him in 1994 and again in 1995 and it took hours for him to even remember me though we had traveled together on eight trips to Romania just two years before.

When not accompanied by Dean or Dennis, I traveled with Romanian friends and pastors when they had the time, vowing to not go alone unless absolutely necessary in the back country.

At Tilligeste, a pastor from Tarju Jiu and I found a leper colony and ignored the "Quarantined" sign which was dated 1948! He and I went in under cover of dawn, delivering Bibles and tracts to the residents. The Romanian army arrived 5 hours later to arrest me. I was severely admonished, detained and later apparently allowed to "escape" when Gypsy friends arrived and took me from the "buckboard" I was tied to in the middle of a parade ground of what appeared to be an army camp. I got in lots of trouble this trip as well because I was caught pulling a trailer with 25,000 Romanian Bibles near Suceavea. (It was then illegal to have more than one bible, to be for personal use) The Officer demanded I "unload the trailer" and I told him to unload it himself as they were Gods Bibles and not mine! (I was very tired) He let me go. The Pastor with me was not cited as I acknowledged I alone was responsible for the Bibles.

Proceeding back to the Suceavea area, we assembled and passed out more bags of clothing and food. Recipients were selected by observing the amount of laundry hung out to dry on their balconies in the massive government housing complexes. From the street, we would get an idea of which apartments had large families. Then we would go inside and simply knock on the door of each of the designated apartments and hand a large sack of clothes and food to whomever answered the door. If asked, we simply said that it was a gift from Jesus. The sacks would contain an assortment of clothing for 10 to 12 children, a canned ham or meat, large cheese loaf. Hershey bars, aspirin and other items. The sacks were the size of an Army duffel bag. In a day's time, we would give away 50 to 60 bags. At one apartment, the lady who opened the door stated to me that she did not wish clothing or food or money, but desired to have us go pray for her son Mihail. I asked what the problem with her son was and she said he was dying. We immediately agreed to go pray for him. One of the other children led us out into the countryside to the grandparents farm. There in the barn the boy laid on a bed of hay, covered with a red blanket. We found the 14-year-old boy to be in perilous condition. We were told he was struck by a car while walking home from working in the fields next to his horse drawn cart. Tragically, this is a common occurrence in Romania. People work the fields late into the night and the carts are rarely with lights or reflectors. Farmers carry a flashlight which they "flicker" at the last moment when a car approaches. The young boy was suffering gravely from many injuries. His pelvic bone and right leg appeared crushed. There were lacerations to his chest and open wounds throughout most of his upper body. His skin smelled of rot, and the odor was putrid. The presence of pus suggested he had been laying there for some time. The grandmother explained that they had no access to treatment or medication because they were just peasants. He was placed in the barn so that his brothers and sisters would not see him die! I knelt next to him and anointed him with oil and prayed. It was heartbreaking to see this young boy left abandoned to die alone in a barn in a world where medical treatment should be available to everyone no matter what your station in life. I prayed and witnessed to him as best I could for nearly an hour until I was exhausted. Leaving him was one of the hardest things I had ever done.

That night, I again got on my knees with my face to the floor and again cried out to the Lord. He again repeated the same vision of airplanes coming from Seattle, filled with medical supplies and assistance. A week later when I returned to Seattle on Wednesday afternoon, my pastor invited me to speak at the evening service. I told them of Mihail and of the necessity for us to do so much more. The idea that we had so much waste in our country and so many in need elsewhere haunted me. After the service, a visitor came up and handed me a small brown bag, explaining that it contained medicines for Mihail. Curiously, no one had seen her before at our services, nor have we seen her since. I had no idea who she was or how she knew about this young boy in Romania and his needs before I had even spoken in the church. I gladly took the bag of medications and shipped it air express to friends in Bucharest with a request that they get it to the Pastor in Suceavea. I included a letter of instruction for the Pastor. It was several years later in Suceavea that I learned the bag consisted of creams and salves. Instantly. I am told, his wounds healed when the creams were applied! They said he told everyone how "an angel came down and touched him, praying and applying medicines". He later went on to seminary, and now he is pastoring a church in Moldova!

Returning to Seattle, my efforts to obtain supplies for Eastern Europe were bearing fruit. The Internal Revenue Service issued its declaration of our 501(c)3 status as a nonprofit organization so that we could now receipt tax deductible contributions. The State of Washington approved our articles of incorporation and the Caleb Board was staffed and functioning well. We had obtained prayer support throughout the community. Many hospitals and medical societies, started providing contributions, including Group Health Cooperative of Puget Sound, the second largest medical association in the country. Other providers included Swedish and Providence hospitals of Seattle, Virginia Mason Hospital, Bremerton's Harrison Hospital, St. Joseph's Hospital of Bellingham, Mary Bridge Hospital in Tacoma, and the University of Washington Medical Center. MedTec Corp. of Texas sent boxes of medical supplies, as did the good Samaritan Hospital system and Portland's Shriners Hospital. Clothing donations were received from many members of several local area churches, and consignment shops. Later, the Visiting Nurses Stores of Southwest Washington donated all of their clothing with each change of season so as to rotate their stock. With the help of many friends and volunteers, we were trucking in donations from all over the Northwest. Two rooms of our church Sunday school were donated to Caleb for storage along with my garage, garages belonging to several of my friends, and several rented storage units, provided to us at a reduced rate. We received some very large donations as word spread, occasionally including the entire contents of a dental clinic in Bremerton, x-ray machines and equipment from medical facilities, dental chairs, and upon the retirement of two dentists, an entire clinic. The Seattle head start program gave us surplused school chairs and tables. Through Bridge Ministries, we received wheelchairs, gurneys and medical appliances. Providence Hospital donated two steam sterilizer machines for medical room equipment. Northwest Medical Teams provided us with surplus equipment from their stock. Christa Ministries World Concern gifted us 16 pallets of infant medicines and vitamins. From Pediacare we received cases of medicines and supplies. World Vision provided distribution of surplus supplies to Caleb Ministries every three months, including computers, office supplies and equipment, soaps and shampoos and school materials.

A local Bank gave us their computer equipment as it was replaced.

But my letters to airlines for shipping were not producing the desired results. Generously, Trans World Airlines, and Scandinavian Airlines (SAS) shipped cargo loads for free on a space available basis to Vienna but this required my having a representative in Vienna to receive the goods and arrange transport from there into Romania. Recognizing this need, SAS generously provided me free travel to Vienna from Seattle from 1993 through 1997.

The commercial cargo shipping on the airlines required items be packed in duffel bags or uniform sized containers and a complete inventory be submitted to the airlines, five days in advance. We were permitted up to 20 duffel bags per flight. Friends with pickup trucks helped deliver the cargo to Seattle, Boeing Field and Everett fields.

One of the early nightmarish experiences occurred when SAS advised their safety inspector requiring us to remove an inventory item listed as "nail polish remover" because of its potential hazardous nature. Going out to the airport at four in the afternoon, I unloaded the 16 duffel bags and plowed through them on the tarmac. After several hours in the heat, I found a little packet of an item labeled "nonflammable nail polish remover"!It was not a problem in shipping and the bags were then loaded on the airplane. I then instructed my people to be more specific in their compiling of the inventory.

We decided the larger items we were receiving required our shipping cargo containers by vessel instead of air cargo, though I refused to let go of the Lord's vision of airplanes flying supplies from Seattle. We had been donated four large x-ray machines, physical rehabilitation equipment, 29 surplussed industrial sewing machines from the Seattle schools, and approximately 60 computers. These items were too heavy for the free shipping. we were being donated from the airlines. We decided cargo containers could be used as well as the airplanes.

Ordered through CoCo Forwarding, we received and filled our first cargo container in 1992, in the parking lot of a storage facility in Burien. It took many pickup trucks and willing hands to assemble the items from all over the Burien area as we packed them into that first container. Because of the need for medical care for women in Romania and the absence of good medical facilities for women in most of the country, Caleb sent their first container to a woman's Hospital in Oradea, Romania. The second container shipped in 1992 was designated for Pastor Ile Trian and shipped to Petrosani, containing a complete dental office, furnishings for four Sunday school classrooms, pine paneling, a library with bookshelves and textbooks and clothing and food supplies. The third container of the year was assembled in the parking lot of Church by the Side of the Road and was designated for the work of Inasmuch Romania Ministries in Bucharest, operated by Ron and Sue Bates.

We continued using the airlines and to look for a better facility for coordinating supplies for cargo containers. In 1993, another container was assembled in Burien, and we then moved our operation to the Arlington air field. Trucking the supplies 60 miles north was cumbersome, but they provided us with free storage and use of their open hanger space. It became clear, we needed a more convenient location for assembling of cargo containers. Our friends at CoCo Forwarding, inspired somewhat by Caleb adventures, closed their office and left for the mission field themselves! When the fourth container at Arlington Airport was shipped, we were offered the services of Northwest Medical Teams in Portland for our assembling and packing. Three more containers were completed there, one designated for Odessa, and another for St. Petersburg and a third that was shipped to Mexico.

1992 and 1993 saw great growth in the Caleb ranks as many volunteers came forward, each adopting our philosophy that no one was to be paid for their services and all of our work was done in the name of Jesus to His Glory alone. We had compiled a listing of names and addresses of large families in Romania who needed assistance. Using the Sunday school rooms during the summer months at LifeFlow Christian Center Church, we held a food drive and collected other items including first aid cream and bandages, vitamins, pencils and paper, shampoos and soap, toothbrushes and candy. One hundred forty-four 16 sq foot boxes were shipped direct to families in Romania and Bulgaria that summer. Each box was 4ft.$^3$ in size and weighed approximately 50 to 80 pounds. The postage and customs duty was prepaid by Caleb so that families did not have a financial cost at the other end. We enclosed letters with prepaid return postage for the families, along with photos of the people assembling the contents in our church. We received many appreciative responses. In 1993, we did the same project by handing out the information to families and having each adopt a family or two as their recipients and preparing the boxes in their own homes. St Elizabeth's Episcopal Church in Burien and Sacred Heart Catholic Church in LaConner joined in the project. Some of the families continue to this day with our mailing project.

Towards the end of 1993, a cooperative was formed of 42 Seattle area ministries to attempt to encourage and assist each other in our chosen area of service throughout the globe. Frank Anderson, whom I had known since grade school, donated the use of a warehouse in the Burien area for the joint use of the 42 ministries. A monthly fee of $10 was established for administering expenses by the Christian Resource Center or CRC, as it was called. Caleb paid its monthly fees and used the warehouse extensively, moving its assembling and shipping process to the local warehouse.

Only one of the other ministries used the warehouse and that only for a short time. The facility became the assembling point for the Marine Corps toys for tots campaign in December 1994., the only other agency to use it as intended by the donor. The CRC disbanded the next year when its director and founder moved to Florida. The use of the 1400 ft.[2] warehouse was then given by Frank Anderson and his business with his uncle Jessie Anderson, A & A Associates, exclusively to the use of Caleb ministries. Located in the basement of a commercial building, the warehouse was originally used to repair vending machines. It has poor lighting or street access but was more than adequate for our uses. Truckers would pride themselves on backing in the 40 foot high-cube rigs, or, they would give up after several tries and another trucker sent out. It was in this unlikely spot that Caleb grew into the mature Ministry of assembling and shipping goods to the entire globe! We are eternally grateful to A & A Associates for sharing the vision with us, housing our projects without cost, enduring many inconveniences to their own operation all these many years.

At the request of the Marshall foundation, we were invited to donate medical supplies and toys and clothing for children in Kazakhstan, to be placed upon the President of Kazakhstan's Boeing 747 airplane, being refurbished at Paine Field in Everett. We accepted the challenge and, using pickup trucks, we arranged a caravan and took supplies to Everett one long Friday, packing them into the airplane, filling the entire passenger area. The president of Kazakhstan was so impressed with the gift for the children of his country that he sent back a letter of appreciation to Caleb Ministries, inviting us to visit his country at any time as his royal guests. He also sent back his airplane for a second load, and we filled it as well.

About the same time as we were gifting Kazakhstan, we became involved in a project restoring a World War II Troop

Carrier. The ship I believe called "Arctic Polar" had been used for several years as a fish processing vessel in Alaska since being surplusded by the Navy. The owners then donated it to a ministry committed to bringing Jews from Russia (St. Petersburg) to Israel. Recomissioned "The Restoration", the vessel first visited Seattle from Alaska for installation of new engines and refitting its mechanics for the trip to Scandinavia where final preparations were being made. The crew put out the call for supplies, workers and whatever could be done to help while it was in Seattle for two months. Ironically, we received a donation 15 days before of 300 crates of surplussed toilet tissue from Seattle hotels. They consisted of partial rolls removed from rooms when complete rolls are installed for new guests. When the crates were offered, we had no idea how we would apply them to our ministry. Then when "The Restoration" arrived with its needs for accommodating endless passengers, we knew the tissue would be a welcome gift to them! Caleb Ministries supplied much of the equipment and provisions for the infirmary and delivered loads of medicines of its own and from Northwest Medical Teams in Portland, at their request. We worked evenings rebuilding and painting parts of the ship. Through contacts at Fort Lewis, we bought 200 beds and bedding from the army and installed them with the help of others in one of the quarters. The ship then continued on across the seas and since reportedly has been making trips every two weeks or so from St. Petersburg to Tel Aviv.

# Chapter 14

# A Dream Realized

*Ps 138:1-139:1*

*I will praise thee with my whole heart: before the
  gods will I sing praise unto thee.*
*2 I will worship toward thy holy temple, and praise
  thy name for thy lovingkindness and for thy truth:
  for thou hast magnified thy word above all thy
  name.*
*3 In the day when I cried thou answeredst me, and
  strengthenedst me with strength in my soul.*
*4 All the kings of the earth shall praise thee, O Lord,
  when they hear the words of thy mouth.*
*5 Yea, they shall sing in the ways of the Lord: for
  great is the glory of the Lord.*
*6 Though the Lord be high, yet hath he respect unto
  the lowly: but the proud he knoweth afar off.*
*7 Though I walk in the midst of trouble, thou wilt
  revive me: thou shalt stretch forth thine hand
  against the wrath of mine enemies, and thy right
  hand shall save me.*

*8 The Lord will perfect that which concerneth me:
thy mercy, O Lord, endureth for ever: forsake not
the works of thine own hands.*
*KJV*

Caleb was beginning to increase dramatically in size and scope now that we had a home warehouse. Operating the offices out of a bedroom in my house, we no longer had goods scattered throughout the area in garages and storage sheds. It was no longer necessary to marshal a convoy of pickup trucks each time we packed a cargo container.

Each Monday and Friday mornings from 10 to 15 volunteers would show up to work sorting the clothes and medical donations. In Romania, Caleb was now supplying assistance to over 30 orphanages located throughout the country and working to build churches across the land. From Greci to Aionca, we were constructing edifices from the ground up, some on our own and others in partnership with local congregations. In Petrosani, Braila, Bucharest and Neamt, we were assisting local congregations in realizing their dreams for a church. And in the greater Braila area, we were encouraging and supplying the means and tools to the Romanians to reach out to the heretofore shunned gypsies. At Braila we gifted $10,000 for purchase of the previously rented church building and its surrounding grounds. The result was a compound which housed a Caleb warehouse, an apartment, a bakery and the church itself. Built by the Braila church, this facility became the staging area for outreaches across the country and even into Bulgaria and Moldova. The Braila Church has birthed 14 other churches including five Gypsy churches. At Greci, we funded $25,000 for purchase of a farm, conversion of the farmhouse to a clinic for treating leprosy and other illnesses, creation of pea-patch gardens for the local community, drilling of a well open to the entire community, and construction of the church.

From the Braila bakery, leftover loaves of bread were taken to the gypsy villages and spread out on blankets, along with boxes of clothing and toys shipped from Seattle. The Braila church then conducted evangelism in the open-air. As a consequence of this work, there are now gypsy congregations meeting at the Lacu Sarat, The Port, Laurali, Lonca, and The Colony! Further, the Braila church itself enjoys a mixed congregation of Gypsies and Romanians, employing Romanian and Gypsy pastors in the services. Caleb Ministries has been privileged to participate in the baptism of hundreds in the Braila Danube, Gypsy and Romanian alike.

One Saturday we went to the village of Greci, known for housing lepers since medieval times in the wilderness east of the Danube. At Greci we preached in the new Caleb built church. It is beautiful. A girl greeted us with flowers and as we arrived Sister Lupita was singing a beautiful hymn that echoed into the streets through the white marble finished front, a color previously forbidden in a village known for having Lepers. It is the most beautiful structure in the village! The adjoining farmhouse had been redone to house Sister Lupita and up to 7 patients in nursing care. Livestock is being acquired, the spring garden is planned, and the fresh water well is used frequently. Incidentally, many of the residents including sister Lupita proudly sported new clothes from our Caleb container. Sister Lupita died a few years later having served gloriously in this tiny village.

In 1994, a telephone call from a local aircraft manufacturer invited Caleb to ship medical supplies, free of charge, to Eastern Europe and throughout the rest of the world on company planes designated for delivery of aircraft parts. This was the vision the Lord gave back in 1990 in the small farmhouse in Suceavea! The dream had finally been realized. We gladly accepted their offer, and for several years, boxes of supplies were delivered to the local Romanian, Bulgarian and Hungarian airfields and picked up by our friends and partners at Inasmuch Ministries and other Caleb affiliates. Caleb now shared office space with Inasmuch Ministries in Bucharest. Using Caleb vans, we delivered their Braille Bibles to the school for the blind in Bucharest and we purchased a Braille printer from England for their use in producing the Bible and booklets for the blind in Romania, Moldova, the Ukraine, Bulgaria and Hungary. We also partnered in their program of caring for and feeding children living on the streets of Bucharest. The approximately 200 children lived amongst the steam pipes beneath the Norte Gaard Railway station. Each afternoon, workers from Inasmuch Ministries cooked soup, cocoa and sandwiches for the Street kids! Caleb paid for the food as its tithe to the Lord for donations received in the USA. Also providing clothing and medical care for the children. One unique donation received by Caleb consisted of a truck load of new shoes and sneakers. They had violated a US patent and were impounded by the federal court in Seattle and returned to the wholesaler with instructions that they could not be sold or distributed within the United States. They were donated to Caleb ministries, and we in turn shipped them to Romania and were able to bless the street children with state-of-the-art shoes. It was a very special day for me when I was able to hand these out to street kids, who had little hope of ever receiving any new clothes, let alone fancy sneakers!. The street children responded well to Ron and Sue Bates, at one point handing over to their care three infants who had been born beneath the streets of Bucharest. The children were raised literally in the offices of Inasmuch Ministries and Caleb Ministries in the coming years. On several occasions I was privileged to accompany the workers from Inasmuch ministries to work with the street children. They took me down into their "houses" they created beneath the streets by using rags and cardboard to separate sections of the steam pipes and vent shafts. It was not without risks. On another visit one kid stole my wallet while I was giving sandwiches to the others. When I chased him he cut my leg with a knife and I backed off. The others then chased him and retrieved my wallet for me, explaining he was not part of their group and didn't know we were helping. Sadly, over the years many of the children we met succumbed to disease, aids, sickness, malnutrition or violence. It was heartbreaking to see these children so determined to stay out of state institutions that they elected to live in the natural elements. But there were many triumphs as well as we saw many grow to be productive individuals. Sixty-six entered the "Jesus Loves Romania" orphanage we supported but most elected to remain free on the streets. At one point the street kids suffered extreme violence when Molotov cocktails were thrown down into their holes at night to try to run them off. Several young boys were badly burned. Through mechanism of a hidden videotape set up we proved to the authorities it was a few security guards for the railway station that prepared and threw the torches and they were prevented from doing this outrage further. Negotiations with the Railroad solicited a promise to donate a small hotel to Caleb and Inasmuch for the children but later the government interceded and took it back. Similar feeding programs have been participated in by Caleb ministries in Iasi, Constanta and in Braila.

On one visit to Bucharest I accompanied Sue Bates out to the streets to serve homemade chicken soup, hot cocoa and bread to the children. I met with the one young gypsy boy who was suffering severe pain and had been refused treatment at the local hospital, a common event. We had him examined by a nurse and it was determined he had several std infections causing extreme pain. Through the nurse I was able to provide medication and antibiotics to him plus a new pair of shoes and a large winter coat. He and his girlfriend were very grateful and promised to attend church. The following afternoon at the street ministry church there they were. The street children developed their own informal church service, held on Saturdays in a vacant lot. They clearly responded to the instructions and lessons taught by Sue and Ron Bates over the years. Being independent in nature, they did not wish adults to spoon feed them lessons but rather performed all of the functions of a church service using their own members and providing their own lessons. Even singing songs and entering into worship time! It was an amazing sight to see Jesus working in the lives of these otherwise abandoned children. Each have their own varying reasons for not wanting to return to their family if they had one. This year the street children feeding program was stopped in Bucharest by the government and Inasmuch Ministries moved their facilities out of the city to a rural setting to put distance between their housed children and the temptations of Bucharest streets.

In 1992, while in Bucharest, we were approached by a gentleman asking our assistance in delivering radio broadcasting equipment for the establishment of a "bandit" Christian radio station, broadcasting from his apartment atop the same building where our offices were located. We gladly obliged by bringing equipment in from Vienna and Budapest and other equipment from Bucharest. After six months work, he began broadcasting Christian music and programming from his apartment into downtown Bucharest. To our knowledge, this was the first fully 24 hour Christian radio station operating within Romania, albeit illegally. Later, several Christian radio stations began broadcasting under licensing. He was never apprehended to our knowledge and it was a privilege to help him get started!

We started reaching out to gypsies first from Braila. We preached in town, as did three visiting Pastors who came from Suceavea to see our work with gypsies. At the town service, many came forward for anointing and prayer and several reported healings. Following church we collected bread and clothes from the Storehouse and Caleb Bakery and went to Llonca Gypsy village. The Suceavea Pastors came with us. Reaching a tiny sod house in the country down a long dirt road, we found a gathering of about 50 gypsies. Spreading blankets out on which we placed the bread, honey in plastic bottles and clothing from the warehouse, we simply started singing and then I preached and then a brother from Suceavea. Several neighbors watched us preach and then joined. There were turkeys running around, chickens, cows, dogs, and even a pig. It was one strange sight but beautiful as well. The people were wearing clothes from the Caleb containers. We saw UW Husky shirts, Mariner caps, Starbuck cups, etc. We passed out Bibles and offered the food and clothes, visited and ministered to them, and had a grand time. Each monthly visit resulted in larger crowds until we found ourselves baptizing 68 gypsies in the Danube! The first such event was difficult because a village spiritualist told them they would be paralyzed for turning their backs on family traditions. We spent hours teaching and responding until the candidates were satisfied. We returned to Braila pretty tired, the Suceavea pastors going home, now convinced Gypsies can be evangelized! I agreed to go to the late night prayer time at the Braila church. When I arrived I found all those who had been prayed for that morning returned with others! During prayer I was asked to preach again and then we had healing service again. Afterwards, we were asked to visit a family in a village who had an illness. We arrived to find the husband paralyzed in arm and leg and in severe pain. As we prayed for him the wife confessed she needed our help as she beats her husband in anger and frustration. (Disoriented, he urinates out windows and uses potted plants, etc). I spent about an hour with her in counseling and prayer, redirecting her anger and taking away her broom and replacing it with a pillow (to hit, not throw!) It is clear they very much love each other and she has consented to get further counseling from Pastor Streghor. Years later the couple are still together and doing very well. Because I am from outside their community, I believe many will confide needs to me they are reluctant to share with others. Under communism, people were encouraged to spy on neighbors and report to the authorities. This fear still exists in many of the older generation.

When I started travel to Romania without the assistance of Vladimir, I flew to Vienna, and there hitched a ride through several different church organizations. On some occasions, members of my morning prayer group accompanied me but most trips I went on my own. I attempted to lease vehicles in Vienna, but found they were unwilling to permit me to use their cars in Romania. On one occasion, I reserved a car from budget rent a car and pre-paid it in Seattle. However, when I reached the Vienna Airport, the budget agent refused to let me have it when I said I was going into Romania, even though that was my stated reservation. They agreed it would be no problem if I were traveling to Yugoslavia, which was in civil war at the time, but they would not permit their car to be used in Romania. We telephone several churches and a member of The Brethren Church agreed to let us use his van in a change for our paying for a lease car for him. This was agreeable with Budget Rent- a -car. When I spoke of this at a Rotary meeting in Burien, months later, one of the Rotarians arranged for me to rent vehicles through Fritz Nekkam, a large auto broker in Vienna and a brother Rotarian. On subsequent trips, we simply e-mailed to the dealership advising the size of vehicle we would require. When we arrived in Vienna he arranged for us to use his personal van for travel throughout Romania. We are very appreciative to the Rotarian brothers and for Fritz Nekkam dealership for the many journeys they made possible.

# Chapter 15

# Brothers In Christ

*1 Peter 3:15-22*

*15 But sanctify the Lord God in your hearts: and be ready always to give an answer to every man that asketh you a reason of the hope that is in you with meekness and fear:*

*16 Having a good conscience; that, whereas they speak evil of you, as of evildoers, they may be ashamed that falsely accuse your good conversation in Christ.*

*17 For it is better, if the will of God be so, that ye suffer for well doing, than for evil doing.*

*18 For Christ also hath once suffered for sins, the just for the unjust, that he might bring us to God, being put to death in the flesh, but quickened by the Spirit:*

*19 By which also he went and preached unto the spirits in prison;*

*20 Which sometime were disobedient, when once the longsuffering of God waited in the days of Noah, while the ark was a preparing, wherein few, that is, eight souls were saved by water.*

*21 The like figure whereunto even baptism doth also
now save us (not the putting away of the filth of the
flesh, but the answer of a good conscience toward
God,) by the resurrection of Jesus Christ:*
*22 Who is gone into heaven, and is on the right hand
of God; angels and authorities and powers being
made subject unto him.*
*KJV*

In November, 1992, I determined to return to visit my friend Vasile Arhile in the village of Neamt. I had not seen him since the first visit in 1990. The roads had washed out during the winter months so that it was very difficult to find the village but after several attempts Dennis Wilson and I located it. As we drove in, I did not expect the welcome I received. This was a peasant farmer to whom I had given a package of clothes for his children and some food for his family two years before. As you may recall, he in turn offered us some raspberries from his garden.

As we drove up next to the stream along the roadway, Vasile spotted me from up in his yard on the hillside. Before our van had stopped, he came running towards me with his arms in the air yelling "God is good, God is good, my friend returns, God is good!" He ran through the stream and up to us were he gave me a big embrace. I've never felt so welcomed in all my life. Ushering me across the log so that I did not fall in the river, he took me by the arm and led me to his house, now completed with two windows and a door. Once inside, he had me sit on the platform bed next to the ceramic fireplace, removing my shoes to warm my feet. It had been very cold and snowy outdoors so he was concerned that I was warm. Parking the van, Dennis had to look after himself!

Vasile then sat across the room in a lawn chair, the only furniture other than the two plywood platform beds. He folded his hands in his lap and began singing songs. The family gathered, six children plus his wife, and kneeling with their foreheads on the concrete floor, prayed thanksgiving for my safe journey and return. His wife then proceeded outside where she cooked a meal of puree potatoes, sausage, and hot tea. Vasile set up the table for Dennis and myself, bringing in two concrete blocks for us to sit on. He then served our meal to us, asking repeatedly if it was sufficient and fussing that he had no napkins or table covering. It was awkward visiting without an interpreter but we made it through well. After we ate, he escorted us through the village to show everyone his friend had returned! We visited at the village Pastors house and then returned to Vasiles family, giving them gifts of clothes and food and funds to purchase a cow for milk for the babies.

The following summer the road was washed out so I could not reach his village. It was disappointing to return to Seattle not having reached Neamt village. Then in the middle of December I received a telephone call at 2 AM. It was a lady from Petrican, the next town to Neamt. She said Vasile had sold his cow to get funds to pay her to travel to the city of Roman to telephone me and tell me not to try to reach his village in the winter as the danger from avalanches was too great! Wow! I knew I had to make it back to see him the following spring.

Traveling with Gigi, a Romanian from Petrosani, we made it back to Neamt in March. Again, I was escorted by Vasile across the stream to his home, placed on the bed and wrapped in warm blankets next to the stove. As he was singing, I asked my friend what he was singing to me and he told me it was Psalms. He would stop once in a while and recite a short prayer of thanksgiving and then continue on with more Psalms. After about 10 minutes, two of the older boys came in bringing a large basin of warm water. They placed it at my feet and began washing my feet as Vasile continued singing, now accompanied by the younger boy. It was apparent that his wife had been warming water outdoors in order for them to wash my feet while he greeted me in this magnificent prayerful manner. The boys offered to wash the feet of my companion Gigi but he declined. Once Vasile had completed his welcoming and we all knelt on the floor and prayed, he once again took me for a walk around the village and proudly showed me the now completed church. While at the church, he borrowed the one light bulb with permission of the Pastor and brought it back to his home so that we had light for the evening. He told me all about the family and what had been happening since my first two visits now that Gigi could translate. He now had eight children, and his wife was expecting the ninth. He had received two large boxes of food and medicines from us for which he was most grateful, pulling out the cardboard containers which he had saved!

The pastor asked that we preach in his church that evening which was quite the honor in this village. Following the service, we returned to his home where his wife had prepared a humble dinner. When you dine as a guest in Romania, the man of the family serves the meal while the wife prepares the dishes in the other room or outdoors. Gigi and I sat at the table set in the large living room. Vasile did not dine but rather looked after our needs. The first course was again a dish of potatoes mashed with water but no salt, pepper or butter is we would have prepared mashed potatoes. The second course was a loaf of bread. In his effort to provide three items as is the custom in entertaining guests for a meal in Romania, Vasile provided two glasses of water from the well, asking as he set the glasses down whether or not it was a sufficient meal. Clearly he and his wife had provided all they had in their home to feed their guests and I responded "it was a wonderful meal and beautifully served." We ate just a little, knowing they would feed the children and themselves later with what was left. It was very hard times in Neamt and food was scarce. Only cabbages and potatoes were available. Vasile was working as a tenant farmer and helping others build or roof their houses or bring in their crops. He had sold the cow because he could not afford the feed. From the proceeds of $120 he paid the lady $60 for the trip to Roman to call me about the dangerous travel and with the remainder he bought a goat for milk for the baby. I gave him $200 when we left along with candy, food and clothes for his family.

He asked if we would stay the evening in his humble house and but Gigi declined. It was a very poor village and he was concerned for our health, so we moved on but I promised next trip I would stay overnight with Vasile and his family.

In the fall, Gigi and I returned to Neamt to see my special friend and his family, now with 10 children! Staying the evening, Vasile made up the one bed for me that was close to the ceramic fireplace and the one on the other side for my friend Gigi. The children were sent to sleep with neighbors and his wife slept on the concrete floor in the second room where food had been prepared, though cooked outdoors. His oldest boy slept in our car to protect it from being vandalized. I discovered the next morning that Vasile had slept outdoors wrapped in blankets on the front stoop to be sure we were safe and not disturbed through the night. I was overwhelmed at the extent to which he went to protect and provide for us in his home. There was frost in the morning and it was very cold! His boy was breaking the ice from the well to get water to wash and clean our car while Vasiles' wife was boiling water over the campfire for our coffee even before getting the children up! She heated a second container so we had warm water to wash and shave. Breakfast was again puree potatoes, bread and onions from the garden. I am careful dining in villages as human waste is used as fertilizer and runs the risk of several diseases from the crops so I generally only eat cooked vegetables. At Vasiles' the "restroom" is a simple plank wall moved about the garden to give privacy from the house. Later, he constructed an outhouse but again its location is rotated throughout the garden.

The following year, I again returned to Neamt. The news was not good. His tenth and eleventh child had died, the girl being stillborn and the boy of pneumonia. He had taken the boy, age 18 months, across the mountain path to the nearest hospital, about 45 miles distant, but they refused to treat because he had no money! His youngest son was with the Lord for lack of a few dollars for treatment. We visited the hospital and set up an account for treatment expenses for the villagers, monitored by the Pastor. Vasile then took me to his son and daughters graves in the yard where we had a small service. He speaks of his children often with great love for each. He asked me to take two or three of the oldest to America to teach them and provide a trade but I had to decline. They eventually made it to Italy where they work in construction jobs, now that Romania is part of the European Union.

I have since been back many times to his house and on the occasions where I have been unable to make it he has found a way to hike out across the mountains and take the train to some place where I am in order to visit with me while I am in Romania. Once he took the train for six hours to get to Braila to surprise me and on another trip he showed up in Timisoara, three days journey by horse drawn cart! Vaslie and his wife have 13 children of which 11 are left. He continues to make a living hunting in the forest and sawing trees for firewood which he sells to others, tenant farming and working for neighborhood farms. Caleb has provided him with goats and pigs and one cow over the years. He remains one of my dearest friends in his enchanting country.

The many journeys to Romania have provided me with examples of God's completeness in my life in ways I never expected. On one occasion when I was alone in Bucharest

I became very depressed because of the number of poor I had encountered on that trip and our inability to do more for them. With four days until my flight home, I rented a room furnished with a simple wood chair and bed, for three dollars. Sitting in the room at night I felt without hope as my mind raced through the number of needs I saw throughout the land. I had prayed and cried and planned but I thought I had failed God and I could just see no way of being able to provide enough for all of the disparate needs. Unexpectedly, there was a knock at the door. I opened it to find a pastor I had never met before. To this day I have no explanation of how he knew where to find me. He said he was sent by the Holy Spirit to bring me to a prayer meeting! He took me to a large house on the outskirts of Bucharest owned by the gypsy lady Gabylunka, a famous singer and entertainer known affectionately as the queen of the Gypsies. Gabylunka has released many cds and cassettes of her music, is famous throughout the world as one of the foremost Gypsy entertainers. Hosting a television program and making appearances all across Europe and the Balkans, she is an "Oprah Winfrey" in her land. Her magnificent home includes a large room where she has prayer meetings every Monday evening. The American pastor had brought me there for my first visit to her home. While there, evangelist Carl Fox from Florida prayed over me and told me that the Holy Spirit revealed "it was not my job to provide for every needy child in Romania but rather to be a good steward of the Lords bounty that he places in my hands". What a freeing word. A huge weight was lifted from my shoulders. From that moment on I have not been over-whelmed by the needs but rather I focus on the results. The widow's mite is sufficient! He provides in His timing and in His way....but he does not demand more of us than we can do. I have been back to the Gabylunka home on many occasions, even sending three cargo containers to her gypsy villages to help start programs through her associates.

When I returned to Petrasani in 1992 to visit with pastor Ile Tran on my first journey without Vladimir, it was wintertime in the Transylvania Mountains. The family Trian welcomed me and we had a gracious visit after which Ile explained it would not be feasible for me to stay the night in their home as they only had one heated room and 12 Children plus he and his wife crowd in there. However, he made arrangements for me to stay with a new young Elder in his church, Gheorghe 'Gigi' Coicheci and his wife Daniela. We became instant friends as they invited me not only to stay in their apartment any time but also offered to drive me anywhere in Romania on my visits. Gigi worked for the state mines harvesting coal and was in a supervisor capacity with a great deal of seniority. Consequently, on any of my subsequent trips to Romania when I provided him with notice that I was coming, he would secure two or three weeks vacation leave and drive me throughout the country. Inasmuch as he was training for Pastoring, we preached together on many occasions throughout the land. He would interpret for me and we enjoyed growing together in honing our delivery of the Word. We preached on mountain tops and in tiny villages, and hamlets and log cabins, in big cities and Cathedrals, at monasteries and youth hostels! On several occasions we were in small wooden shacks far out in the wilderness with no electricity, using only a kerosene lantern or candles for light. On one occasion we drove along a dry creek bed to reach a church which had no roads leading to it. Those in attendance came on foot, tractor, buckboard or horseback. Gigi continued to travel with me until the Romanian economy turned sour in 1994 and he was then demoted by cutbacks to working the mines fulltime. On our last journey together, we had visited Braila where we met a new friend named Marin Tiripa at the Braila farm owned by the pastor of the Braila church. Marin stated he wanted to help me whenever I needed anything in Romania and to call upon him if I needed anything. Gigi and I then returned to Petrosani where Daniela and Gigi now have six children. I am so grateful for the years of travel with Gigi and for our adventures from all corners of Romania and west clear to Austria, south to Turkey, east to the Ukraine and north to the Polish border! God gave me a servant with a heart to serve when I needed him most. Gigi is one of the pillars upon which Caleb built soundly! Today, he serves as Senior Pastor of the Filedelphia Church of Petrosani, having followed upon retirement of Ile Trian. Gods work is secure in the Transylvania Mountains in his able hands.

On our last trip together, Gigi and I were in Bistritsa in north-central Romania when we ran out of Romanian Lei, the local currency. Our Visit was with a large family with 12 children. We could not purchase motorina (gas) without lei so it was decided the best thing to do would be to go to the marketplace and find a money changer and change dollars for lei. The problem was that this was an illegal transaction in Romania. The army, police and Securitate enforced currency laws with a vengeance and penalties were severe. We went to the marketplace early Saturday morning and there discussed a plan. Our host family could not go in to exchange money because he had 12 children and could not afford to be put in prison if caught. For Gigi, it was the same problem with his wife and five children. They both looked at me. As an American, if I were caught it was likely I would simply serve a short-term and then be put out of the country. We prayed about this and I asked the Lord to give me a sign as to whom I could approach safely about changing money. We knew there were undercover police as well as Army personnel in the crowd.. I then walked about 100 feet into the market-place and started to laugh. Directly in front of me was a very large Turkish man wearing a Seattle Mariners baseball cap! I have been a Mariners fan since they were founded in 1977! I walked up to the man and asked him if he would exchange money for me and speaking perfect English, he said "sure"!

He gave me a great exchange rate and even came out with me to our van and agreed to have his picture taken. When asked about the baseball cap, he said he got it in Istanbul just four days before and he had no idea who the Seattle Mariners were or even what baseball was. He just thought that the cap looked good. I have since referred to him as my "angel money changer".

Later in the summer of 1994, I was working at Inasmuch Ministries in Bucharest and no longer had the services of my friend Gigi from Petrosani as a driver. I had hoped to journey on to Braila by train but took sick and determined to stay in Bucharest for a couple days until I got stronger. I was sleeping on an old yellow bed in a garage where the windows were broken out and there was a severe draft. There was no facility for cooking and there were rats and garbage about the premises. The room was stuffed with boxes and supplies and junk. It was hardly ideal but I was in no condition to travel and the Inasmuch Ministry was packed into temporary quarters while building a new facility. I knew I had a fever and suffered sweats through the night. Suddenly, the garage door opened and in walked the man I had met in Braila just months before, Marin, with and his bride to be, Christina! To this day I do not know how they knew where I was or that I needed help. They literally gathered me up in my blankets and put me in their car along with my suitcase! Without explanation, they took me to Braila and told me I was never to come to Romania again without telling them first so they could meet me at the airport or border. From that day on, Marin Tiripa has been my closest friend and constant companion on every trip to Romania. He is the stepson of the pastor of the Braila farm church. His natural father was placed in prison for assaulting his mother when he was only nine years old. She was severely injured and Marin and his brother and sister lived on the streets for several years. He became very streetwise and possesses insights and understandings of street children and orphans beyond measure. Because of this, he has a natural insight into the thinking and lifestyle of our target clientele has been valuable in expanding Caleb Ministries. When he was 17 the state apprehended him and placed him in institutions, labeling him a dangerous man because of his father' reputation. While in the state schools, they tried every way they could to keep him from being released into the public by insisting he complete all educational and vocational programs. He earned degrees in engineering, carpentry, math, languages, and technology. When his mother spoke out on a national television interview about her fundamental Christian beliefs, he was declared an enemy of the state as her son, even though he was not then a believer himself. He was placed in prison and served two years at Jilava, near Bucharest! From there he was released into the military where he mastered even more trades. His accumulation of talents and insights has made Caleb ministries that much more effective in reaching the poor people of Romania. God could not have given us a better representative to spread the work in the Eastern bloc countries and could not have provided me with a better friend and brother in Christ.

Marin returned to Braila and his mother and stepfather became a believer, and was baptized in the home of Gabylunka a few months later. He is now a pastor, operates a farm and has a construction business. He and his stepfather also are beekeepers and many times over have divided their beehives to share with our new pastors to give them a means of providing for their families while spreading the gospel and growing their churches.

Marin and I have traveled throughout Romania, Hungary, Bulgaria, Moldova and the Ukraine professing Christ in tent shows, churches, evangelisms and crusades. We have visited the sick, delivered food to the needy, fed widows and orphans, and have witnessed countless miracles in the name of Christ. Presently, he pastors the church at Greci and conducts evening services at the main Braila Church plus shepherding the Gypsy Churches at Lacu Sarat, Lauralie, The Colony, and The Port.

On one of our journeys north with Marin I was visiting with a family and they were interested in my early journeys in to Romania. Their son arrived to visit with us for the evening. As I was discussing events in Suceavea in 1990 he asked if I was aware of a tent evangelism program recurring there about that time. I told him I was one of the speakers and he became very distressed. He told me that in 1990 he was working for the Securitate secret police. His unit was ordered to beat the people leaving the tent meetings at night in order to persuade others not to attend. He said the first night they did this he was very disturbed to the point that he told his superior he would not do it again. The next night he was ordered to take his men and repeat their harassment and beating of people. He obliged but then nightmares haunted him and again he told his lieutenants he would not do it a third night. He was ordered but instead he resigned from the Securitate and was sent to prison and then inducted into the military. While serving in the Army he was part of a platoon ordered to destroy Bibles confiscated from Christians. As he picked up one large family Bible and opened it, he discovered the words on the page were glowing as if alive and he became very afraid. He then began to ask others cautiously about this Christ. One elderly man and his wife led him to Jesus. Now nearly 15 years later he asked forgiveness for the actions he participated in during our 1990 evangelism! He was so relieved to be able to unburden his wounds! God works in truly mysterious ways! He related other events where he was visiting with friends over Christmas and carolers came to the door. As they opened the door and listened to those singing, he noticed that one of his former comrades in the Securitate was part of the group, obviously working undercover. As he stared at the man, the man's appearance physically changed and he appeared to be "as a ghost made of ashes or a zombie". He said he looked like death had control of the man's soul!

The Lord has provided many helpers to Caleb ministries in Romania and in Eastern Europe. Marin and Gigi have been as angels fulfilling our needs but there are so many more as well. When I first journeyed to Eastern Europe on my own, I had no idea the scope my travels would take or the dangers I would skirt. I was clubbed by an Orthodox cleric while feeding street children in Bucharest on one occasion. The priest believed that by my feeding and providing clothes for the children I was interfering with God's discipline of them for some sin The Almighty was working out in their lives. The priest broke my rotator cuff with his blow. On another occasion I was arrested and tied by plastic straps to a fence while my vehicle was being searched. On yet another, a customs agent struck me so hard he broke my nose while trying to dissuade me from shipping supplies to gypsies whom he believed were unworthy of gifts or help. But in the protection of Marin, Gigi, and others, I have traveled safely the last five years.

# Chapter 16

# God's Gifts in Bulk

*Ps 144:12-145:1*

*12 That our sons may be as plants grown up in their youth; that our daughters may be as corner stones, polished after the similitude of a palace:*

*13 That our garners may be full, affording all manner of store: that our sheep may bring forth thousands and ten thousands in our streets:*

*14 That our oxen may be strong to labour; that there be no breaking in, nor going out; that there be no complaining in our streets.*

*15 Happy is that people, that is in such a case: yea, happy is that people, whose God is the Lord.*

*KJV*

When Caleb started sending containers to Romania in 1992, we were neophytes in the world of commerce. "CoCo Forwarding" helped a great deal in teaching us the ropes. When they ceased operation in 94, we had to find other forwarding companies. Caleb has established a good sense of the documentation necessary and procedures to follow. Since then, Caleb has freely offered its services to many other organizations in helping them ship containers throughout the globe as well. The procedure for shipment is to first reserve the container through a broker. Then you assemble and inventory the contents to place in the container, checking to see if any is declared contraband by recipient or shipping country. We usually faxed the inventory ahead of time to the customs people so that they could clear the shipment in advance. Then you assemble a work crew to load the container. A standard high-cube container is 40 feet long, 8 1/2 feet wide and 10 1/2 feet tall.

Apart from the precise inventory of items and their value you need to generate the following documentation;

1. Certificate of Donation stating the contents are donated and not subject to sale.
2. Packing List indicating the contents of the container itself including pallets, large items and bulk items.
3. Invoice showing the value of the items being shipped
4. Transport Certificate giving direction to the Port Authority on who the consignee is and how transportation will be made from the port.
5. Certificate of Quality and Conformity indicating the items do comply with requirements of the host country and are not expired or in poor condition.
6. Certificate of Medical contents with a list of all medicines and medical supplies including expiration date and dosage, including Latin names and dosages.
7. For computers and computer supplies, a Legal Opinion Letter stating the items are suitable for export from the United States in conformity with the National Defense Operation Act, not containing computer technology or software currently prohibited by the United States government from export.

8. Certificate of Conformity to Import Regulations stating the items conform with the rules and regulations of the recipient country
9. Certificate of Fumigation and Washing indicating all clothing has been cleaned in water exceeding 130° and all items within the container had been fumigated.
10. Certificate of Conformity of fitness showing there are no pornographic items or inappropriate clothing such as lingerie or suggestive apparel.

Caleb Ministries generated this paperwork for each and every container shipped, and in some occasions further documentation was required by the host country such as regulations in Romania requiring an affidavit assuring our warranty of repair and that we will replace computer parts that failed within 12 years of our importation.

Each container cost from $4000-$16,000, depending upon its ultimate destination. Some purchased containers were shipped as Medical Supply Buildings or offices or housing to be placed on location in the foreign country while others were returned to the United States, sometimes bringing goods made by peasants and widows to be sold with proceeds being returned to those making the goods. From 1992 to 2008, Caleb Ministries shipped 135 such containers to Romania and 35 containers to other countries including Moldova, Russia, the Ukraine, the Congo, Ghana, Nigeria, Mexico, South Africa, Tanzania and Burma.

Computers were donated from banks as they replaced their equipment, schools, businesses and individuals. Each computer was refurbished by our staff of computer technicians and equipped with software including the Bible in Romania language, an office suite program, and internet access. Some computers were networked together for use in orphanages and schools for instruction by Caleb volunteers.

John Stanley and John Worley did most computer engineering for us, both being certified computer technicians.

Some ladies mended garments while others washed and ironed, packed and repaired the donations. Four groups of ladies worked through the weekdays in making quilts, blankets and baby clothes. Another talented lady made dolls and doll clothes, generating beautiful gifts to be given to the children. Gentlemen woodworkers created toy cars. Church staff collected songbooks, hymnals and teaching materials. Entire collections of cassette teachings and programs on cd were sent along with the appropriate operating equipment and convertors for adapting to the 220 Direct Current Romania power system.

Medicines and medical supplies that were requested from doctors and institutions were frequently purchased by Caleb ministries and included in the containers or delivered directly by hand or courier. Mannatech generously provided thousands and thousands of dollars of their products when they became aware of the use Caleb was making of them in helping down syndrome and malnourished children in Romania. Through Manna Relief, their nonprofit counterpart, cases of medicines and vitamins were shipped throughout Eastern Europe and Asia.

The evening before packing of any container, Orkin fumigated "the box" at a gift rate to assist our work. Initially, we paid companies $300 to $500 for fumigation until Orkin came to our rescue, doing the work for just $125.00 and providing proper documentation for customs. The next morning from 20 to 30 volunteers would come from throughout the community to donate their time on Saturday mornings with their only pay being a pizza lunch!

The standard valuation in humanitarian work is that a 40 foot container holds conservatively approximately $250,000 worth of used goods, so we are told. This works out to nearly $42.5 million in medicines, clothes, food, bibles, office supplies, and equipment was delivered by Caleb ministries in just 15 years, our of our modest donated warehouse in Burien, Washington. Incredible and awesome is our God!

The volunteers are the Heart and Soul of Caleb Ministries. Without their support very little would be accomplished. Most are senior citizens or people of modest means who just want to help and serve our Lord. One of the ladies making quilts is blind and relies upon her companions to tell her when to change the color of the materials she is knitting. She travels by senior citizen access bus across town each Tuesday to be part of the group making quilts and blankets. Another lady turned one bedroom in her home into a quilting room where she churned out approximately 60 quilts a month for several years. She died at age 92 after delivering her last batch of quilts to Caleb Ministries at our spaghetti feed.

We assisted a ministry in difficulties back in 1994. This ministry was attempting to duplicate cassette tapes of praise music to distribute around the globe. It had received thousands upon thousands of cassette tapes from an elevator-music company, to be re-used. This required erasing the cassettes of their prior content and removing all labels. One of our volunteers suffers from multiple sclerosis and is unable to walk or control a lot of her muscle movements. She would have me deliver 12 plastic sacks full of cassettes to her apartment each Saturday morning. I would place them on the floor around her apartment as per her instructions.. Through the week, she would crawl around to the cassettes on the floor and erase them using six portable recorders and then peel off the labels. She alone prepared approximately 60,000 cassettes for our re-recording and distribution. We then recorded a set of Romanian Bible stories, worship songs and teachings on 10 cassettes of the refurbished cassettes and distributed them along with Walkmans, donated or purchased at a reduced rate from Fred Meyer stores and Wal-Mart, to people throughout Romania.

When we first started our ministry in Romania we collected the names of many orphans and sick children as we went from city to city. We did this in order to have names to pray for once I returned back home. A lady in our church named Cleo became bedridden with illness. She would ask for my directory of people to pray for every time I came back from a trip. In her last five years she spent literally days in prayer for the children of Romania until she went on to the Lord in 1995. Our ministry is filled with prayer warriors and servants dedicated to helping in whatever ways possible. Every other month we host a big spaghetti feed in my home for all Caleb volunteers and their guests. It is not unusual for them to arrive bringing homeless, strangers, visitors and the sick. There is always room for more at our table. We have about 50 to 60 each spaghetti feed!

On a journey in 1993, our cargo shipment via TWA included a duffel bag containing very important heart medicine requested by a Bucharest doctor. When the flight arrived at Vienna, the duffel bag with it was missing! TWA searched everywhere they thought it might be but it did not show up. The Caleb volunteer continued into Romania. Two weeks later, a companion came in from a flight landing in Bucharest. When he went to meet him at the Bucharest airport, while waiting at the coffee shop (at that time just a plain room with two booths and two card tables and chairs) he found something hitting his legs under the bench. Looking, he found our missing duffel bag! Mind you this duffel bag was suppose to be in Vienna, Austria but showed up in a coffee shop in Bucharest, Romania two weeks later. I have no earthly explanation but I know the doctor was most grateful.

One lady who became a part of our work early on was Edie. Though she suffered from cancer, she always showed up for the work parties and then never failed to take things back to her house to mend or repair or sort during the week. On one occasion she invited a homeless woman from the streets to come to the warehouse and help us fold clothes. While talking with the lady, she discovered it was her birth date. Edie went to the store to get a cake and pop so that we could celebrate the birthday. It was a big surprise and blessed event for the homeless lady. We dined on the loading dock, sitting on boxes of folded clothing and singing happy birthday to this beautiful lady while tears ran down her cheeks. This was typical of Edie's generosity and heart.

I cannot emphasize enough how important the Army of Caleb volunteers is. They have held dinners and auctions and yard sales as well as spending many weekends and weekdays at the warehouse, donating their time to benefit strangers. No Caleb ministry volunteers officers or workers are ever paid for their work And it is all done for the Glory of God alone. It is because of their many hours and their generous hearts that so much has been done. We have been privilege to help start 49 churches throughout Romania, provided relief supplies medicines and gifts to over 300 orphanages, have preached and evangelize innumerable times in many countries, only because of the kind hearts and giving nature of my brothers and sisters in Christ.

On the second journey to Romania in 1990 I was privileged to visit several orphanages as well as remote villages. Everywhere we went, the children were seeking some gift or token. The Lord gave me the idea of creating candy packs to hand out to children. Returning to Seattle, the first candy packs were assembled at St. Elizabeth's Episcopal Church in Burien by members of my Cursillo Ultreya and Bethel Bible study groups. In each zip lock bag we placed four crayons, a matchbox car, five or six pieces of hard candy, a coloring paper of a Bible scene, a coloring paper of John 3:16 in Romanian, and a copy of The Four Spiritual Laws in Romanian language, obtained from campus Crusade. We assembled about 800 candy packs. They became a big hit when next visiting villages. Later, we added personalized buttons which had colorful animals and "Jesus expressions" written in Romanian such as "He Is King", "The Lord Is Coming" and "I Am Redeemed ". The candy pack assembling has become a major event for Caleb volunteers. Each New Year's Eve we meet at our church to assemble approximately 3000 candy packs. We stop at midnight and pray for the recipients and the people in Romania, Eastern Europe, Africa, the Philippines and other lands were Caleb serves. This year, we have been asked to provide over 10,000 candy packs for the Philippines alone.

One of the most memorable trips occurred in 2006 in the winter. Completing my planned trip with Marin, we had assembled 3000 shoe box Christmas boxes from Samaritan's Purse for distribution to the Braila area gypsy villages and churches. We had visited the orphanages and hospitals, distributing our clothing, toys, vitamins and medicines across the land. Journeying across the country four times, we had prayed for many and preached in churches and meetings as scheduled. But with just three days remaining for my journey, I learned of an orphanage in Western Romanian that had no food and no toys for the children for Christmas. They had used their entire budget for medical needs of a particularly ill child and now had nothing left for the holiday season. It was December 17 and I was scheduled to return home December 21. Marin and I decided we must do something to help these people have a blessed Christmas. Using my credit card and the last of my cash, we purchased food from a bulk food distributor. We told the people in Marins' church that we were going to this village the next morning. They stayed up all night baking goods and donating canned fruits and vegetables from their personal pantries for us to take. Cookies, cakes, pastries, candies, it was a beautiful array. Adding Samaritan's Purse Shoeboxes to our load, the car was jam packed. We drove across the country, running out of gas at Bucharest. Marin and I then pawned our watches (his idea) to get money to complete the journey across the country. We arrived and completed our task on December 20th. The children and staff were ecstatic with joy and surprise. Marin then took me to Bucharest just in time for my flight back to Seattle. The best Christmas ever!

It should be remembered that Caleb ministries is non-denominational. We have several churches which have supplied support and given us the platform from which to present our ministry including Westside foursquare Church, Hope Christian Fellowship, St. Elizabeth's Episcopal Church, Shorewood Foursquare Christian Fellowship, Church of the Resurrection Episcopal in Bellevue, The Cross Church, Heart of God Fellowship, Victory Outreach, The Wooden Cross Lutheran Church in Monroe, Victory Church in Sacramento, Bread of Life Mission, Union Gospel Mission, Lutheran Compass Center, and others.

It is a miracle to see God pulling together so many diverse forces in our community into one apparatus by which many are blessed across the world.

# Chapter 17

# Expansion Into Africa

*Acts 1:7-12*

> *7 And he said unto them, It is not for you to know the times or the seasons, which the Father hath put in his own power.*
>
> *8 But ye shall receive power, after that the Holy Ghost is come upon you: and ye shall be witnesses unto me both in Jerusalem, and in all Judaea, and in Samaria, and unto the uttermost part of the earth.*
>
> *9 And when he had spoken these things, while they beheld, he was taken up; and a cloud received him out of their sight.*
>
> *10 And while they looked stedfastly toward heaven as he went up, behold, two men stood by them in white apparel;*
>
> *11 Which also said, Ye men of Galilee, why stand ye gazing up into heaven? this same Jesus, which is taken up from you into heaven, shall so come in like manner as ye have seen him go into heaven.*
>
> *KJV*

In 1995, our website, www.Calebgoodnews.org began to draw attention from individuals overseas. One individual particularly interested in our work was Dr. Pastor Jeff Eze of Nigeria. Dr. Eze began writing e-mails asking for more and more information On Caleb Ministries and its programs. He was enthused by the variety of programs and services being performed by volunteers in the name of Jesus. Finally in 1997 He Asked to Affiliate with Caleb Ministries by forming an offshoot in Africa. Our board approved and Caleb Ministries was registered in Nigeria as a nonprofit organization. The young pastor traveled extensively and signed up churches in 14 African Countries as Caleb Ministries affiliates. By 2000, Pastor Eze reported having 644 churches partnered with Caleb Ministries in Africa, stretching from the Cameroon's, Nigeria, Benin, Biafra, Ghana, The Ivory Coast, Sudan, The Congo, Sierra Leone, South Africa, and Spanish Guinea. Since then, we have added Rwanda, Kenya, Liberia and Uganda as additional Caleb affiliates. We have shipped two containers to Liberia, two to Ghana, one to Nigeria, one to The Congo and one to South Africa.

Our program for affiliates requires a church or organization to undertake at least one anonymous charitable event in support of homeless, widows and orphans, prisoners, physically impaired, or otherwise forgotten peoples, a minimum of each six months. Some of the programs included feeding and visiting prisoners and providing fresh water for them, providing food and clothing to homeless and refugees, buying milk and medicines for Chelsea House programs for polio victims, establishing computer classes to teach office skills to teens, restoring homes of elderly, providing assistance to flood victims, and refitting wheelchairs and prosthetics for physically impaired people. All is to be done in the Name of Jesus and without any remuneration to the providing Caleb affiliate. The number of churches and organizations joining Caleb Ministries continues to grow worldwide with new affiliates joining from Pakistan, Bangladesh, Myanmar, India, and the Philippines.

In 2006 I had the privilege of ministering with Dr. Jeff Eze in Biafra, Nigeria and Ghana and to officiate at the swearing-in of the Caleb Ministries Board for Africa and addressing the first graduation class from the two Caleb Good news Schools of Theology In Nigeria and in Ghana. Respectively. Flying to Lagos, and then 10 hours by very crowded and cramped bus to Enugu, we visited many churches and outreach programs. At Chelsea House we presented additional computers for the polio victims and met children named "God's Glory ", "Rose of Sharon ", "Emanuel's child ", and "Wheels of God ". At the Red Cross center we gifted the home with a TV set for the staff, boxes of powdered milk, pediacare products, and fresh fruits and vegetables, sacks of rice and clothing and toys for the children. In the plaza we met many local people and distributed gifts of boxes of food and medicines designed for individual families.

At the Zion Temple a five day evangelism was held after which I was surprisingly and ceremoniously presented with the title "tribal chief" and given a chieftains robe handmade for me in the chief's home village. We met privately with refugees and political leaders in exile including Biafra martyrs asking us to pray for their family and anoint their homes for protection. Our accommodations were Spartan but more than adequate. I felt very at home amongst the Africans. Church services were exciting and the worship time lively as they celebrated our Lord in dance and song in ways I had not witnessed elsewhere before. Clearly they knew and loved the Lord as much as any others on the planet. Following the inauguration ceremony and swearing-in of the African Caleb Board, we witnessed to prisoners at a local high-security facility. With 44 graduates from the seminary, we proceeded to the local prison at four in the afternoon. It was unbearably hot and the end of a very long day, having preached three sermons and officiated at the inauguration ceremonies. Once inside the prison compound, I was advised by the chaplain that only I could address the inmates and that those with me were not allowed to interact with prisoners. The prison cells were made of stone with heavy bars over the window openings and door entry. The cells were approximately 6 feet wide and 6 feet deep constructed entirely of stone and iron, with poor ventilation and lighting. Each was serviced by one bucket for food and one bucket for waste. Many of those imprisoned were of different nationalities and did not speak the local Obo dialect, isolating them further in their imprisonment. It was explained that the crimes consisted of anything from theft of bread or a chicken to harden criminals incarcerated for murder and rape. The difficulty for the inmates was that under Nigerian law one could not be brought to trial for their crime until they had procured an attorney to advocate for a hearing or trial. Their family had to obtain counsel to bring their plight to the attention of the court. For those who had no means to pay a lawyer, they were simply trapped in jail. We were told many had served six or seven years for a simple crime of theft of food because their family could not afford to hire counsel or were unaware they were even in jail! Some of the inmates were very young and most were dressed simply in a loin cloth or briefs. In preparation for our visit, Caleb sent a gift of two trucks of fresh drinking water to the inmates for four days prior to our visit because the area had been suffering drought and good water was in short supply. A concave concrete platform in the yard was suppose to catch rain from which they filled their buckets but because of the drought it had been dry for a month!

The chaplain addressed the prisoners first, chiding and admonishing them for their folly of being locked up. He called upon them to throw themselves upon the mercy of God. He addressed them by standing in a hallway facing the cells which were arranged in three dormitories situated in a triangular configuration. He would run back and forth down the hall yelling his message and it would be repeated in different languages by inmates yelling out from their cells. He then invited me to address the prisoners. I quoted Isaiah 49 versus 9-16 in reminding them that God knew of their plight and still loved them and still wanted to help them in making the best life possible given their circumstances. He cared for them to the point that he wrote their name on the palm of his hand at the time of creation so that he would never forget them. I told them they were loved and we were praying for them and we knew God loved them no matter what they had done, as a father or mother sorrows for their child. I implored them to turn to God and seek solace in Him as He is their creator, father, savior and deliverer. This message was repeated over and over throughout the dormitories as shouts from men speaking different languages and dialects rose across all three buildings.

As I was leaving the compound and crossing the yard, I heard a commotion coming from all of the surrounding rooms in the three dormitories. I could see hands raised sticking out the bars towards the sky. I asked Dr. Jeff Eze what they were saying. He replied that they were crying out their name to God and saying "it is I, Japheth, here I am Lord; do not forget me", "here I am Lord, it is Roberto, please still love me", "remember me Lord it is Egun, I am still here Lord". I was overwhelmed that the Holy Spirit gave me a meaningful message to deliver to these men. Returning to the United States, I contacted a number of civil rights organizations in order to enlist their help or at least support in getting people to represent the imprisoned in African jails but received no response. As a Caucasian, I was informed my presence would not be welcomed or trusted In the Nigerian Court System. I still write letters seeking help for these 806 men and 81 women.

In the spring of 2007 I once again joined Dr. Eze in ministering in Africa. During the first week we had the pleasure of going to villages and remote encampments where we had church programs. One such visit was to Emene, a six-hour drive to see the home village of Dr. Eze and visit his home church and mother. They were very pleased because no one had ever taken the time to come to their remote village though Jeff had provided invitations to many. Then visiting Enugu in Nigeria and reacquainting friendships with the pastors there, we journeyed by private car north to Benin, Ghana and Togo. Evangelisms were held twice-daily in Togo with good response. Bishop Peter Ani provided the host church for most of the services. On Friday evening we held a healing service in Lome Togo and the Holy Spirit touched many. The church held about 300 but before the evening was over we had people lined up on the streets coming in to be anointed and prayed for. There was dancing and praising God in an awesome display of love for the Lord. The next morning I was picked up at my modest rented room by a pastor declaring he had been sent by Dr. Eze. He took me by private car to a small church outside of town to minister to his congregation, though I had been expected elsewhere. I had been effectively abducted by friendly capture so that their church could be part of the crusades. Once I figured this out I shortened my message and hailed a cab and returned to town where I found Dr. Eze and the members of the bishops church waiting in the street for me. I was flattered but not amused by being detoured to another church. I found my driver had been bribed $50 to go along with the subterfuge.

Following six days in Togo, arrangements were made for the trip back to Lagos for my flight home to Seattle. The only travel available in that area of the world was by hiring private car. We had to leave Togo, and cross Benin, into Nigeria. At crossing each border along the poorly maintained two-lane road included graft requiring to pay bribes together with delays occasioned just because you were a foreigner. The roadway is dotted with burned-out vehicles, abandoned property and remnants of violent events. There are little shanty stores most of the way with very few conveniences and no police protection. The best road conditions are in Benin but that is a short part of the trip. The officers and authorities at the border required I purchase a visa in order to depart their country even though I already had a visa in my passport. Their explanation was that the one I had affixed to my passport "could have been a forgery". This cost an additional $80. At the Benin border for entry into Nigeria the authorities required a new visa because the one I had affixed to my passport was issued by a previous government authority allegedly "no longer in power". This cost $120. The immigration officer at Benin insisted I be searched completely to be certain there was no contraband. Basically, it was a strip search of person and belongings. The result was that they became aware I had $1000 US in my case which I was saving for my return flight from London to the United States. 45 minutes after we left the Benin border, it was dusk and we were assaulted by bandits on the roadway. Wedged between vehicles on the narrow dirt and rut roadway, a white panel truck turned broadside directly in front of our vehicle forcing us to be pinned in the middle of three "lanes". Two men exited the white panel truck and began firing automatic weapons in the air. At the same time, two men approached on motorcycles from the rear, also discharging weapons into the air. One of the two on the motorcycles appeared to be one of the officers from the border station we had just left a Benin. I was seated in the passenger seat in the front of our little Honda vehicle with two cases of Coca-Cola on my lap and luggage on top my feet so that I could not even move. I was the only white person within miles. In the back seat of our car were Dr. Jeff Eze, a lady singer from Spanish Guinea who was accompanying our evangelisms, and a stranger who had hired a ride from our driver from Togo to Lagos. The driver started yelling immediately. One of the bullets struck the window frame directly in front of my head and the second creased the passenger door at my side. The stranger in the back seat whom had secured a ride from the driver, immediately got out of the vehicle among the flying bullets and quickly examined the situation and started yelling instructions to the driver in the Obo dialect. The driver followed his instructions and nudged our car to the left off of the street by shoving the other out of the way. He then drove into a drainage ditch and around the front of the white van, into a small grove of trees on the right side of the road. Dr. Eze banged on several doors of shacks asking for refuge but no one obliged. The gunmen kept shooting in the air, robbing the passengers in the car that had been in front to our right. We waited in the bushes only about 15 feet away until it was pitch dark. The bandits wounded several people and threw Molotov cocktails into the vehicle directly behind ours on the road. Because the traffic had cleared in front of the white van we assume they thought we had gotten away by going ahead and they then were pursuing our phantom vehicle somewhere towards Lagos in front of us.

I turned to thank the gentleman in the back seat who so bravely exited the car to find an escape route for us. He was gone! Neither Dr. Rev. Eze nor the driver or any of the other passengers could tell me anything about the man. He simply disappeared!

Continuing on into Lagos, we received a cell call advising that people were waiting for us at the airport in Lagos to offer refuge. They had become aware through radio broadcasts of our being attacked. When we got to the airport I was introduced to a lady described as the Queen of the Ogbo tribe! She offered me the hospitality of her large luxurious home, including body guards. Escorting me to her house. She provided me a hot meal, cooking it herself, and comfortable lodgings, even though the power was out. She insisted the guards move a generator so that it could operate a fan and small light for me in a bedroom and she heated water so I could wash. The next day she gave me a personal tour of Lagos in her vehicle and introduced me to many important people in the town. That evening, she escorted me to the airport herself in her private car while her security escorted us in the following van. As this Queen of the Igbo people, 25 million worldwide, carried my luggage, she shoved the airport guards back and told them she was their queen and they would not interfere! She marched to the airport counter and instructed British Airways they were to provide the best arrangements possible for my flight! Bishop Peter Ani arrived from Togo to see me off as well. My departure from Africa was quite the sight.

My plans to return to Africa in 2008 had to be canceled with the sudden passing away of Dr. Pastor Jeff Eze. We were very sorry to learn he died suddenly of a fever. He was only 37 and left a wife and five young children. Dr. Jeff Eze was a great servant and Minister and a Blessing to Caleb Ministries. He will be sorely missed but certainly is now with our Lord. Bishop Peter Ani represented Caleb ministries at the funeral services and Dr. Jeff's brother Eze Chibuzo has assumed the directorship of our African ministries. This summer they received Rwanda and Liberian affiliates and are conducting medical missions in the Enugu Region.

# Chapter 18

# Caleb Down Under

*1 Sam 12:24*

*24 Only fear the Lord, and serve him in truth with all
your heart: for consider how great things he hath
done for you.*
*KJV*

In 1995 members of the Pentecostal Union of Romania
approached Caleb Ministries and asked our assistance in initiating Romanian style Pentecostal churches in
Australia. They offered to provide airfare and support for
our helping launch charismatic church programs for the
many Romanians who had immigrated to Australia under the
Ceausescu regime and since it's fall. Reportedly, there were
approximately 5000 Romanians residing in the Melbourne
area, taking advantage of the open immigration policy of the
Australian government and its help extended to Romanian
refugees through the communist years.

Pastor Nikolai Ianos of Timisoara ventured to Australia
on a six-month work visa to establish a church in Dongadong,
just outside Melbourne. He invited Caleb to attend the inau-
gural services and undertake evangelism as a kickoff to the

church. With great pleasure, we accepted. Our first trip to Australia was a great success. The services each evening produced healings as worship unquestionably was pleasing to the Lord. Besides the Church of Pastor lanos, we were invited to conduct services at Sunshine Church, 7th Avenue Pentecostal Assembly, The Church of England Assembly which hosted Romanians, and at the Salvation Army Center. Apart from services, we assisted in providing legal advice to Romanians undergoing immigration hearings and to provide testimony in support of the persecution still being faced by many in their home country of Romania.

In 1996, I returned to Australia and again preached in many services and interactive church programs. We were invited to conduct evangelisms in the outback and to minister to aborigines and gypsy populations. It was an exciting outreach. The Romanians residing in Australia determined to assist in the reconstruction of their homeland by sending containers of goods in the Caleb fashion. We worked with Grace Missions and doing documentation and export licensing and in clearing containers received in Romania through the port at Constanta, on their behalf. The Australian Romanians concentrated on sending appliances and electric goods because the Australian standard was the same 220 direct current circuitry employed in Romania. This removed the necessity of our shipping large electronic appliances from the United States which required converters to operate on the different current system.

By the next year, Pastor Nikolai Ianos decided it was necessary for him to return to Romanian to care for his family. His church in Dongadong was becoming too fundamentalist for the Romanians immigrating into Australian society and he deemed it best to return home. Six other Romanian churches were growing and meeting the needs. Following the final two weeks of services at Dongadong, we embarked upon one last evangelism and crusade across Australia. Launching the program at Melbourne, we moved on to Dongadong and Victoria and then to Sunshine. From there, we traveled to Sydney and the Salvation Army Center where we held programs for three nights. Following, we held programs in Brisbane, Perth and the outback. It was an exciting time. The Dongadong Church continues under new pastorate as do the other Romanian Pentecostal Churches. In 1997 a Romanian friend of mine moved to Perth where he established a new Romanian Pentecostal church with his family of 12 children and his wife. They commenced their ministry on Christmas day by inviting people from the town to a Christmas dinner in their home, a boat. They telephoned me in Seattle so that I could be part of the unique celebration.

In 1998, I visited pastor Nikolai Ianos in Detroit where I was honored to jointly officiate for the wedding of his youngest son. It was a huge ceremony attended by over 1000 and followed by a sit-down dinner. The bride is the granddaughter of Lydia Rascol, a Romanian lady who lived in the United States and then return to her native country to set up a mission serving the poor in Negreste, Vaslui Province. Caleb is proud to be a sponsor of Lydia Rascol who at 86 years young provides food, clothing and Mannatech vitamins for over 200 poor in Vaslui Province.

The same year, I learned that the oldest child of a pastor friend was imprisoned in Timisoara for working with Christian agencies in the villages two years before. The charges were clearly fabricated to punish the Pastor and his family and were outrageous. I determined to visit the young man in prison once I heard of his plight. Leaving Braila by car with my friend Gigi, we headed towards Timisoara. We slept in the car the first night but it was frightfully cold and we determined to not do so a second night. Arriving at the town of Allesed at midnight, we looked for a place to stay. There were no hotels or motels and no Inns or hostels. We decided to go to the Pentecostal church to ask their help in finding a place to stay. We saw a light on in the sanctuary and entered. There was an elderly man kneeling in prayer at the altar when we arrived. He looked up at us and we told him we were headed to Timisoara to visit a friend in prison but that we needed a place to stay for the night. He asked whom we were going to see and we told him. His face showed surprise and amusement but he said little. He invited us to his modest one room apartment across the courtyard. There he served us some chorba soup and hot tea with bread while he made up two beds, one on the floor on a mat. Then he explained that he is the grandfather of the young man we were going to see in prison! In a country of 24 million people and nearly 200 miles from our intended visit to the prison, we had found the grandfather of this young man. Alleluia, God is good! Arriving at the prison, I was not permitted to see my friend as he had had a visitor for the month, his wife. They were allotted only one visit each month and that under severe controls. So, I wrote a letter to him encouraging him and letting him know he was in our prayers. Nine years later when I visited his family, he had been released and was now living in England. But the family had not forgotten my attempts to visit their son. They put together a surprise barbecue lunch (in winter!) and then momma pulled out the letter I had written her son while he was in prison and read it aloud to all there! She had kept it all those years. I was very moved.

On another visit, I arrived on the doorstep of friends in Constanta without any prior notice to them that I was coming. There was no postal service or telephone service or any other reliable way of letting them know ahead of time I would visit. I had six guests with me and it was the middle of winter and snowing heavily as I knocked on the door. The lady opened the door and welcomed us in, explaining that the Holy Spirit had told her four hours before we were coming. She had bathed the five children and put them to bed early and had borrowed enough milk from the neighbors in order to prepare 7 cups of hot cocoa for her expected guests.

The Lord looks after his own in the mission field. Traveling alone on one trip, I arrived at Magedea looking for the family of Cornelius Constantine. Knocking on the door of the house I believed to be his, the lady answered and I asked for my friend. She said he would be coming home later and that I should come in and get warm. Once inside, she prepared a hot meal of Chorba soup and bread and tea. After I had eaten, she advised that she did not know Cornelius Constantine or his family but that I looked like I was hungry and needed a good hot meal and place to get warm. Such is Romanian hospitality. I learned later Cornelius and his family had moved many miles north. Addresses and street signs are inexact in Romania, often intentionally misleading to thwart strangers and invasions, and often simply because such niceties are low in priority in struggling economies. Asking locals does not help much as most do not know much beyond their immediate circle of travels. Most are aware of the block they live on but not much beyond their town as travel was very limited under communism and required special documents and passes even to go beyond your village.

Jesus works in mysterious ways and his wonders never cease to amaze me. On another occasion I visited a family that was very distraught because there little girl had been removed from their custody while at the school. They were not told why nor where she had been taken. Because children are the "property" of the state, authorities felt no necessity to explain to the parents in this situation. Simply put, the authorities decided the child needed to be removed from the family for some unexplained reason and did so. The mother and father were beside themselves with fear and anger and had no idea what to do next. We prayed about their child and the Lord showed me that we would know where she was within three days and that she would be found safe. I assured them she was in His care. The next day I had to leave for Bucharest, some one hundred fifty miles away. While there, I was working with fellow missionary Ron Bates when he suggested we visit hospitals to pray for people. I agreed it would be good. Then he asked me to pick a number as there were seven state hospitals in Bucharest, each known by a number. I picked number two and we proceeded to the state hospital Number Two. There we had to register with the police on the second floor in order to have access to the patients. While we were filling out the paperwork I noticed the young girl who had been removed from her parents two days before, I spoke with the doctor and he explained that she was removed because they thought she was mentally ill, as she lashed out with her arms and hands constantly and yelled. I explained that she had a hearing difficulty and that we could have it corrected if they would release her to go to a clinic with us. They agreed and we took her to a free medical clinic where we had been supplying medicines and apparatus for two years. They performed a simple surgery on her ear and she regained her hearing. We were able to return her to her family two days later. We paid a total of $60 for the transport, services and medical implants necessary to restore her hearing. Whenever I return to Romania now, I am treated by the family is if I were royalty. But I am simply a son of the King.

Driving in the town of Petrosani one afternoon, a lady ran in front of my vehicle to stop me in the street. When I got out she begged me to help her boy Bogdan. He was two years old, and suffered from fainting spells whenever he exerted himself physically. He was unable to play with other children or to maintain himself without help and constant supervision. The problem turned out to be impairment in the valves in his heart. Contacting several organizations, we found help from Healing the Children Foundation in London. After making application for surgery, they flew him to London where heart surgery was successfully performed. Today he is very healthy and his family is most grateful. Caleb works with many organizations throughout Romania and other countries and has in turn provided services and supplies to those organizations in return.

Another young boy in the same town two years later was reported to have been in a coma for 60 days. The parents asked for our visit to anoint and pray for the boy. When we did so, he immediately woke up and has been normal ever since. We do not know what caused the coma nor do we claim that we in any way healed him. It is the power of the Lord only that heals, and we are but his instruments or conduits for prayer. We simply follow the commands in James 5:13-20. It is a blessing to be used in the smallest way and to see His love extended through us to others.

A later trip took us to Timisoara where we learned a friends wife was in the hospital with kidney damage and wished us to pray with her. At 10:30 at night, we found our way in to the dialysis unit where five ladies were undergoing care. The hospital facility was very basic with the waste being removed by a hand pumped apparatus and with little hope of success. As we prayed with our friend, the other patients asked we pray with them. A Doctor came in, saw us and turned and left, locking the door! I thought for sure he was heading for security but we just continued praying with the ladies. One knew her time was near and asked for forgiveness and peace. Another lady spoke only German but said she understood what we were doing and clearly understood my prayers, as I was speaking in tongues. Another said she had not accepted Jesus until that moment! The last lady said she had not prayed since she was 14 years old! It became an incredible time of prayer and preparation. After two hours, the Doctor returned and said he saw the guards coming in the hallway and had locked the door to keep them out as he realized what we were doing!

It is not possible to detail all of the miracles and unexplained events the Lord has done in my life in the mission field. Clearly, he blesses those who serve him and he provides in ways the world could never understand. If I have learned anything, it is the importance of stepping forward in any situation, following the lead of the Spirit, praying each step of the way, expecting miracles, and fully and totally trusting God.

# Chapter 19

# Visiting The Pacific Rim.

*Ps 62:11-12*

*11 God hath spoken once; twice have I heard this;
that power belongeth unto God.
12 Also unto thee, O Lord, belongeth mercy: for thou
renderest to every man according to his work.
KJV*

We have always been interested in expanding Caleb to other areas of the world. Our blessing has been to provide clothing and medical supplies to people taking them to the Navajo Indian Reservation and Yakima Indian Reservations, missions serving Eskimos in Alaska, street ministries in Seattle and Portland, and shipping goods to Mexico, Belize and Southeast Asian countries. In 2007, we were invited to participate directly in programs in The Philippine Islands. A local Seattle ministry called Heart of God Fellowship operates a program called Morningstar which serves a mission at Abra in northern Luzon Island, The Philippines. Several Caleb volunteers were also serving in the Morningstar program and were acquainted with the mission and program at Abra.

Frequently it was our pleasure to provide supplies to Morningstar for their shipment to The Philippines. Then in February of 2007, I was given the privilege of accompanying a mission team to Abra for two weeks. To make the time more effective, arrangements were also made for me to serve in the community of Santa Maria, approximately 100 miles south of Abra for the subsequent two weeks with a local Church Community headed by Pastor Marben Lagmay.

At Abra, The Heart of God Mission was a great surprise and delight. Similar to many of the missionary programs we support in Romania, this facility houses young people and orphaned children and babies, performs outreach evangelism to the community, provides hygiene and health care programs and parenting classes to local people; has educational programs for the youth, and clearly is serving the Lord in many ways. Caleb was pleased to supply computers for Internet access and training programs and to forward medications and vitamins for the health care. We sent boxes of clothing and toys as well as candy packs and educational materials. In 2008 we contributed funds towards purchase of a van for the mission. It is our pleasure and good fortune to be a supporter of the Abra mission in the Morningstar Ministry. We continue to ship approximately 10 boxes a month plus monetary support to their programs.

Santa Maria was a wonderful surprise as well. Once I arrived, I became partnered with a local pastor, now a bishop, who enthusiastically and relentlessly has set upon a course to evangelize not only the Philippines but Southeast Asia. His church became my home as I slept in the office and lived in the facility for the next two and one half weeks. He maintains a Bible college with approximately 26 students who are working their way towards pastorate credentials. These young people were a huge blessing to me and their enthusiasm, participation and interest in spreading God's love. Each had been assigned three or four remote villages as their responsibility. Their job was to conduct Bible classes and programs for the young people each week in their villages and to take the message of the Sunday morning service to the village during the afternoon and evening hours for those who could not travel to town. These young associate pastors had done a wonderful job in preparing their people to receive God's word and embrace his love. Once I arrived it became my responsibility to present the gospel in a way that would invite the villagers to accept Jesus into their lives. I did this by witnessing of what Jesus has done in my life, giving my personal testimony.

Each morning, we had a church meeting at Santa Maria. Following that, for the afternoon we would venture to one of the villages, usually one without electricity. Some of the young associate pastors had already arrived when we got there, setting up the sound system, bringing chairs from the church, and preparing food to serve to the people. When we arrived either by motorcycles or tri-cycles (sidecars), rugged terrain jeepneys, by walking or by canoe, we were greeted by music led by the young pastors. With great enthusiasm and obvious love, they brought the crowds attention to the message to be presented. With the local senior pastor trans-lating, I presented my testimony of what the Lord had done in my life. Following this, Pastor Lagmay would present the altar call and most everyone would come forward to formally receive Jesus in their life. Once he gave the sinners prayer, each person was anointed and prayed for. Then we presented the candy packs to the children and proceeded on to the next village for an evening service. At the next village, lights were strung in the trees to illuminate the setting. The sound system and the chairs had been moved from the previous village and were already established by the time we arrived. The same program of worship and testimony was presented with the same result. On Sunday, Bishop Lagmay began the day at 4:30 AM with a service for shopkeepers, 10 AM service for the regular church, and then to village services to round out the day. Often, we took time for a wake, to visit the sick, to instruct the pastoral candidates, or to visit other dignitaries. This routine consisted of three services each day with four or even five on Sundays! The result was that after 15 days, 1720 people arrived at the Philippine Sea for baptism in The Name of Jesus!

In 2009 I returned to the Philippines and spent one month working with the same senior pastor and his pastoral candidates, visiting many more villages deep within the surrounding mountains and towns. We presented computers and medical supplies to state clinics and to medical programs operated by local people. Caleb Ministries is blessed with unique resources in providing these supplies. We spend approximately $1800 per quarter in purchasing medications and we acquire many thousands of dollars worth of donated medications from other sources which we send to doctors in the Philippines, Romania, Bulgaria and the Ukraine. The last visit included reaching villages far in the mountains occupied by rebels, unavailable many months of the year due to the jungle road conditions and monsoon rains. It has been a unique opportunity and a blessing beyond description to work with these people in The Philippines. They have in turn sent out missionaries to bring the other churches and communities into the Caleb family in Taiwan, Vietnam, Belize, South Korea and Indonesia. They have plans to reach Filipino churches in the Hawaiian Islands and throughout the world. God has blessed us richly with this new outreach.

# Chapter 20

# Our King Is Coming-
# There Is Much to Do

*Rom 12:1-6*

*12:1 I beseech you therefore, brethren, by the mercies of God, that ye present your bodies a living sacrifice, holy, acceptable unto God, which is your reasonable service.*

*2   And be not conformed to this world: but be ye transformed by the renewing of your mind, that ye may prove what is that good, and acceptable, and perfect, will of God.*

*3   For I say, through the grace given unto me, to every man that is among you, not to think of himself more highly than he ought to think; but to think soberly, according as God hath dealt to every man the measure of faith.*

*4   For as we have many members in one body, and all members have not the same office:*

*5   So we, being many, are one body in Christ, and every one members one of another.*

6  *Having then gifts differing according to the*
   *grace that is given to us, whether prophecy, let us*
   *prophesy according to the proportion of faith;*
KJV

As Caleb Good News Ministries reaches its 20th anniversary, expansion is underway with seven affiliate churches in India and one mission in Adak, Alaska coming into the umbrella of programs supported by this modest Burien ministry The phenomenal growth in the global outreach is testimony to the Lord's blessing of this unique all volunteer organization If it had transformed into a profit venture or started paying salaries to those undertaking its work, it is doubtful they would have succeeded. Because of the heart of the ministry and its desire to be of service for God's Glory alone, He has endowed it with the wings of eagles and sent it from the east to the west.

There have been stumbling blocks and learning curves along the way. Anyone desiring to enter the mission field is cautioned that there are untold hours of loneliness and doubt, many frustrations and unexpected hurdles. You must be adaptable to succeed and you must listen to the Lord's direction and heed it at all times. I have been shot at, stabbed, jailed, beaten and left without food or heat for days at a time, robbed, cheated, lied to and abandoned in rural fields. Yet, it has been so worth while seeing The Lord provide!

The most exasperating part of working in the Third World for this missionary has been the continuous 'promise' that larwe turned out to be past 'hopes', and not sureties. By that I mean, frequently people will tell you what they will do or what they will pay or where they will be and it does not come true. But when confronted, they assure you it was there "sincere desire" that they were voicing and, if they had the means, they would have come through. You hear assurances for example that if you provide $5000 they can complete the church within four months! In the West we would accept that at face value. The $5000 is granted and then applied by them elsewhere. When you return and ask about the church you are told that it was "a hope" they had but totally outside the realm of possibility for various reasons. In fact, they look at you funny for having believed it was ever possible! The $5000 was appreciated and applied in other areas which you cannot deny are good needs but they were not what you had intended. Not having your own staff on site is a problem so you stop funding projects, but the experience has cost you in level of trust. These disappointments can sour you or can cause you to grow. Caleb made mistakes certainly, but for the most part they have turned into learning experiences. Only one project we were promised did not get completed within budget, though some took longer than anticipated. The point is do not be surprised to find Third World People are often desperate and will tell you anything to get funds or supplies. Love them through it, check on their application of any funds you provide, demand receipts, and supervise the projects. We have helped construct 49 churches in Romania, all within budget, only one of which was not completed.

The disappointments are greatly outweighed when you see the sacrifice they make in the projects they embrace. Their hearts are good but their word is suspect at times. It helps to park your pride at home! It does little good to get angry or upset when things happen that you view as dumb h. For example, on one trip the host asked Vladimir and myself and two others to make ourselves at home in an upstairs bedroom. He then left, locking the door behind him! The four of us were locked in the room for 9 hours while he went to work! It served no purpose to get angry, though we had no bathroom, food or form of entertainment. It is at times like this when you learn patience and talk with the Lord! His reasoning was he was afraid we might leave and get lost or hurt or not return. On another occasion, for five days my trip was postponed because my host was waiting for his visa clearance to travel to Moldova. Each day as I waited packed and ready to go, he would come and say his visa was not yet approved by the police. After waiting five days, finally on Friday, he announced the visa had arrived from the police station. While packing the car, his wife let slip that the visa had been there all week long, but he was waiting for the children to complete school so they could travel with us. When confronted about this deception, he responded "my English is not so good. I do not understand what you say" You are much wiser to overlook the deception and go forward. Remember that you are a guest in their home and they are trying to fit you in to their schedule as best they can. At times their method stinks, but you will get much farther overlooking than confronting.

What we consider good table manners are not the same as theirs. I have had people simply "spear" food from my plate! Salad is often in one bowl of the table from which all eat with our forks. A beverage such as water or pop is freely passed around in one bottle without separate glasses but if you "wipe the lid" before drinking, you are insulting the others! You just grin and trust the Lord to ward off bugs. In some places the locals will share one spoon or not even use utensils when they eat, coupling three fingers and grabbing the food in the hand and tossing it in. Try not to stare or wince. Nursing of infants can be done at the table, in open public places, and sometimes by surrogate mothers such as a grandma or aunt. They will nurse children much older than we do. Just accept the differences and concentrate on being Christ to them and you will go farther. You do not have to adopt their behavior but do not be abhorred or put off by it either. Theirs is a much older culture than ours and has its own richness and heritage. Eating ants, cockroaches, raw pork, dog or cat, raw fish, raw eggs or "Balut" (ducklings about to hatch!) are experiences that will endear you to them if done in good spirits! It is astonishing what your system can handle when put to the test.

After you encounter official "promises" that are untrue. For example, we purchased property from the Orthodox Church and converted it into a meeting place. Two years after the fact, the Orthodox Church complained to the authorities that you are holding their property without just cause because under the Orthodox Church by- laws it is not possible to sell "consecrated" church property. Having developed the property, you refuse to return it. You point out that the by-laws may preclude sale of the church building but that the surrounding land is not encumbered and you own it! After months of struggle a compromise is reached that the building is an historical church site which will not be altered but will be used perpetually by you along with the surrounding lands. In the West this behavior would be treacherous but in Eastern Europe it is a commonplace trick used to get money, but a little inventiveness saved our church compound from being taken away.

You obtain permits to build a facility for orphans and the authorities require each dormitory bedroom for two children to be 16 ft² in size. Once the building is complete you are notified by the authorities that they had changed their mind and the requirement is now each room be 14 ft² per two occupants **and** they require you to **shrink** each room smaller so as not to impair the psychological needs of the children! You begin to believe you have fallen down the rabbit hole with Alice in Wonderland! The kitchen is completed at great expense and the inspector decides he wants three separate storage areas, one for meat, a second one for cold goods, and a third one for dry goods, each divided by barrier walls that are insulated floor to ceiling. Each must have a locking door. The kitchen is remodeled to the inspector's satisfaction and he determines you must provide a staff restroom within the kitchen. You again remodel to provide the kitchen staff restroom and are then advised a separate shower area and toilet must be provided for the head chef. Each visit by the inspector must be paid for and frequently the inspector changes to new personnel from time to time so that previous promises are of no reasonable merit. The state orphanages and institutions do not have to comply to these "changing" regulations. Basically, as a stranger in the land you are without standing to complain and you should recognize the need to participate in "gifting" to those in authority or abandon your project entirely!

Caleb Ministries has not built any orphanages itself but it has helped other agencies and ministries work their way through this tangled web of officialdom. We have seen projects built and completed that remain idle throughout Romania because the authorities continued to throw up barriers that have no merit in reason. Literally millions of dollars have been invested and yet these orphanages remain closed without just cause, while orphans, abandoned children, and runaways sleep in the streets! It is a disgrace and disheartening fact of life. Apart from churches and pea patch gardens, which we deed to the local community, Caleb has not engaged in any construction projects and does not own any buildings anywhere. All of our funds have been used to provide structures that are given to the local congregation as a house of prayer, bakery, school, home, or for the shipping of supplies, purchase of medicines, or procurement of food and goods, which are consumables. We do not own anything. Even our vehicles are given to local pastors to use in our absence with the understanding we can use them on our visits. But we have seen huge waste by westerners for inexplicable reasons. We are heartbroken by what we see as poor stewardship.

For example, one major American denomination literally took a map of Romania and tossed a dart at it to select the location to build a church. They then went to the target village and constructed at great cost a church that will house 300 people. They then assigned it to the Pastor of the village. He had been holding services in his small house for many years. He has from 10 to 16 people each week who attend his service in his small house. The church edifice next to his house is very expensive to heat and to maintain. It is literally too large for the village and has become a burden to the pastor. On our last visit he was considering moving away because the building was too much responsibility, expensive for him to heat and pay electricity, and his congregation was down to 5 people.

It is not an easy thing to enter into another culture and understand it without years of effort. One gift the Lord has given me is the ability to live simply and without modern conveniences. The lack of hygiene or privacy and the absence of what Westerners would consider clean food is not a problem for me. I enjoy becoming part of the local culture and living as they live as best I can. The burden is to return to the west and see all of the waste and all of the luxuries that are so unnecessary to a fulfilled life. When I go into a supermarket after having been on the mission field I literally want to scream. The number of choices and decisions become overwhelming and my conscience starts clicking off images of those who have so little.

These are adjustments you have to make when you enter the mission field. You cannot expect eggs and orange juice for breakfast, privacy in a bath or even a restroom that is any more than a tree at the side of the road. It is a fact of life that the eastern societies have lived this way for years and they do not understand our fetish with cleanliness, privacy or banquet dining. In their lifestyle food is simple and from what is available. It is pointless to complain about what you do not have; rather enjoy and appreciate what you do have. The Romanians are a beautiful people and very devout in their worship of God. That they choose to spend their evenings for five nights a week in worship and prayer should not be a matter of curiosity but of envy! The march of Western-style television across the eastern bloc has been very slow amongst the Christians. In the rest of society the modern conveniences and idiot box has been adopted quickly. This has created a diversity of society in the Balkan countries. The lines between those who have and have not are crisscrossed with lines of those who will adopt Western culture and those who will not. You find a few very rich and many exceedingly poor most of whom are pious, creating richness in the Eastern Church. But rarely do you find the devout Christian electing to stay home and watch television or attend a soccer match rather than being in church for worship and prayer. This is why God's hand is upon the Romanians and this is why you experience so many more healings, prophecies, visions and outpourings than in Western churches. The Eastern have the gifts of God, exercise those gifts, and receive healing, visions, prophecy and blessings. They expect God to respond to their needs rather than demand God to fulfill their desires as we often do.

I would encourage anyone who is willing to give up their comfortable lifestyle, safety, health care, wardrobe, wealth and mindset to venture into the mission field and throw yourselves into the arms of the Lord. There is no greater feeling than to be dependent upon our Creator while serving in his dominion and authority.

He has shown me His love. For all those who have made this possible, the countless Caleb volunteers, sponsors, donors and board members, I am eternally grateful. I can do nothing of myself. It is only by the support of many that I am able to go forward and only by the consent of Our Savior that anything good comes from my mere pursuits!

Again, I urge you.....as Paul did....

*Rom 12:1-9*

*I beseech you therefore, brethren, by the mercies of God, that ye present your bodies a living sacrifice, holy, acceptable unto God, which is your reasonable service.*

2 *And be not conformed to this world: but be ye transformed by the renewing of your mind, that ye may prove what is that good, and acceptable, and perfect, will of God.*

3 *For I say, through the grace given unto me, to every man that is among you, not to think of himself more highly than he ought to think; but to think soberly, according as God hath dealt to every man the measure of faith.*

4 *For as we have many members in one body, and all members have not the same office:*

5 *So we, being many, are one body in Christ, and every one members one of another.*

6 *Having then gifts differing according to the grace that is given to us, whether prophecy, let us prophesy according to the proportion of faith;*

7 *Or ministry, let us wait on our ministering: or he that teacheth, on teaching;*

8 *Or he that exhorteth, on exhortation: he that giveth, let him do it with simplicity; he that ruleth, with diligence; he that sheweth mercy, with cheerfulness.*

9 *Let love be without dissimulation. Abhor that which is evil; cleave to that which is good.*

*KJV*

# Here is my Americanized recipe for Chorba:

CHORBA (Peasant soup)
2 shredded heads cabbage
2 big onions
5 carrots
1 rutabaga
grate the above........simmer in oil until yellow

add
water
sliced big mushrooms, chicken, pork or turkey (about 4 cups, in big chunks, or bones if no meat available)
1 cup Borsht

add
6 cups diced potatoes
1/2 pint sour cream
7 egg yokes
1 to 2 cups white vinegar for sour
simmer..... 5 hours
serve hot with heavy white bread or potato bread
as garnish add sour cream, lemon or vinegar to make more sour to taste......

CPSIA information can be obtained
at www.ICGtesting.com
Printed in the USA
BVHW071123141119
563832BV00001B/64/P